VISION
FOR A
NEW CIVILIZATION

VISION
FOR A
NEW CIVILIZATION

•

Spiritual and Ethical Values in the New Millennium

•

Edited by Chung Ok Lee

Won Buddhism Publishing
New York, U.S.A. and Iksan, Republic of Korea

VISON FOR A NEW CIVILIZATION

August 2000

Copyright ©2000 by Won Buddhism Publishing
Book design by Suin Jang
Cover design by Eun Young Lee
For information address: 431 East 57th St. New York, New York 10022

Library of Congress Cataloging-in-Publication Data
Vision for a New Civilization
Edited by
Chung Ok Lee
ISBN:89-8076-017-5
1. Ethics-Values-Religion-Spiritual-Philosophy-Psychology
2. United Nations-Civilization-Global Affairs
3. New Paradigm—Societal Change
Printed in the Republic of Korea

Contents

ACKNOWLEDGEMENTS

We wish to thank The Committee of Triple Universal Ethics of Won Buddhism who generously funded *Vision for a New Civilization: Spiritual and Ethical Values in the New Millennium*, in honor of Master Chung-san's Centennial Anniversary of his birth. We also wish to thank the Won Buddhism Press for their generous service in publishing this book. We offer our heartfelt thanks to family, friends and colleagues who inspired us and supported us in presenting our ideas to the public.

FOREWORD

I welcome the invitation to write this foreword. I have been closely associated with the activities of non-governmental organizations in the area of ethics and values. They have an important role to play in the work of the United Nations, governments and society.

Those who practice their own ethics and values make a contribution of commitment and wisdom. Whether in government, business, civil society, communications, trade unions or international organizations and other walks of life, we all face the challenge to practice our personal values in our professional life.

We know it is not easy, yet every leader, every policymaker and everyone of us is capable of listening to our heart and conscience when confronted with a major decision in personal and professional life. We know that stable communities are organized around commonly accepted standards that reflect shared values of different societies, cultures and spiritual traditions.

The world of today has introduced increasing tensions between the individual values we hold dear and the decisions we have to take driven by increased market competition, reasons of state, national or specific interests, power politics, and more generally, conflicting demands coming from a wide array of stakeholders.

This book is about the role of ethics in our troubled world. It is a multidisciplinary effort and a new vision on the part of well-known experts in their respective fields. The articles in this book, taken together, form a remarkable and refreshing

new way of thinking and approaching the work of global
institutions and governments as well as individual life. They
invite us to leave aside moral indifference and dare to demand
an ethical compass from the powers that be as well as from
ourselves.

Ambassador Juan Somavia

Director-General, ILO
and former Chairman of the Preparatory Committee of
the World Summit for Social Development

The Challenges of Our Times

Humanity faces great challenges on a global scale in this new millennium and is called upon to deal with increasingly complex problems in our interdependent world. This book examines spiritual and ethical values in the work of the international community in the new era. It presents new visions and ideas for a new civilization from many different perspectives. It is encouraging to see that there is an emerging vision of universal ethics emanating from many different disciplines including political science, philosophy, ethics, religion, spirituality and psychology.

This new vision calls for humanity to move beyond the boundaries of nationality, race, ethnicity, ideology, religion, and gender to meet on common ground in order to build a world of happiness and prosperity.

I believe that peace and justice will not be attained until we come to universal ethical agreements. This book invites everyone to participate and engage in building a better world together. It offers new ideas and brilliant new thinking on how to change our lives individually as well as our institutions collectively in order to meet the global challenges of our times.

Rev. Kim Sam Yong

Chairman, the Committee of Centennial
Anniversary of Master Chung-san's Birth

INTRODUCTION

We live in a new world, one of rapid and profound transformations whose contours are still unclear and whose direction is clearly pointing to the slow emergence of a new civilization. The forces of regional and global integration are at work exerting their strong impact on humankind, its institutions, and its environment. The uncertainty in the individual's life, the questioning of societal values and institutions, and the prevailing sense of pessimism appear to mask for the moment the great promise of the future.

The authors of the following chapters are inspired to participate in the outcome of the great transformations taking place in the 21st century and in the eventual ascendancy of universal values and human cooperation in the resolution of humankind's vital issues. They see the emergence of a new civilization as enunciating the advent of new forms of global relations and their humanization.

While recognizing the serious crises in the world today, we believe nonetheless, that the 21st century brings with it unprecedented opportunities for humankind to join hands to effect positive changes in our global society and to help reduce the intensity of those crises. We are convinced that such changes would come about if every member of the world community consciously made the moral commitment to contribute to the great task of laying the foundations for the new civilization.

Chapter One presents a common framework for the ethics of the 21st century in the light of the importance of ethics based on a broad analysis of the current global crisis. The author formulates four clusters of ethical values and principles that together would be adequate to meet the global challenges.

Chapter Two examines the newly initiated dialogue among civilizations at the United Nations and offers an analysis on the nature and scope of this dialogue. It underlines the intrinsic capabilities of civilizations in participating effectively in the resolution of major world problems and in strengthening human solidarity.

Chapter Three suggests that the constructive role of religion today is to develop its primary language as well as to build a language of public discourse. Civilizations face the same challenge. Interreligious dialogue can provide a model for dialogue among civilizations.

Chapter Four discusses the transformational impact of evolutionary changes in the external world and the parallel internal changes of consciousness needed to direct these evolutionary changes for the common good. It analyses the consequences and radical differences between old and new paradigm world views.

Chapter Five analyses the new civilization and a more humane world order from a historical perspective of social transformation. It includes a comparison between the theories of civilization of Samuel Huntington and Arnold Toynbee.

Chapter Six examines relevant spiritual and religious teachings and interprets them in the context of the contemporary world. It provides a spiritual, ethical and religious basis to transform individuals, communities and institutions toward a new civilization.

A COMMON FRAMEWORK FOR THE ETHICS OF THE 21st CENTURY

Yersu Kim, Ph.D.

Dr. Yersu Kim was the Founder of UNESCO Universal Ethics Project, and the former Director of the Division of Philosophy and Ethics, UNESSCO. He is also the Vice-President of the International Federation of Philosophical Societies and a member of the International Program Committee, XXI World Congress of Philosophy. He has been a professor of philosophy at Seoul National University. He was born in Seoul, Korea. He received his B.A. from Harvard College and his Ph.D. in philosophy at the University of Bonn. He is the author of many books and articles in linguistics, philosophy and ethics.

The future cannot be a continuation of the past and there are signs...that we have reached a point of historic crisis... We do not know where we are going. We only know that history has brought us to this point.

Eric Hobsbawm, The Age of Extremes [1]

---

[1] Eric Hobsbawm, *The age of Extremes* (New York: Vintage Books, 1996) p.584-585.

PROSPECTS FOR A UNIVERSAL ETHICS

I. The Global Crisis

1. The Globalization of Problems

We stand at this century's end in a situation of extraordinary openness. The forces of the techno-scientific economy are threatening the very foundation of human life, even while they create unheard-of material bounties for a minority of humanity. These same forces are giving rise to ever more complex social, political and moral questions. At the same time, the old ideas and institutions that had served humanity so well over the past several centuries in its tasks of survival and flourishing seem increasingly irrelevant, unimportant or even counter-productive. People are abandoning old loyalties and building allegiances shaped by rapidly shifting ideas and hopes. The last part of the century is, in the words of an eminent historian, an era of "decomposition, uncertainty and crisis"[2].

The first clear signs of uncertainty and crisis came in the form of the ecological crisis that accompanied the first oil shock in the early years of the 1970s. Politicization of the energy resources by the oil-producing countries had abruptly exposed the fragility of the " golden " years of post-war economic development, decades that had seemed to promise eradication of poverty and full employment to almost all the countries of the North and for some countries in the developing world. The oil shock, combined with the ideas of the limits-to-growth writers of the 1970s, highlighted the universal or global

---

[2] *ibid*, p.6.

nature of the crisis. The best known of these documents, the so-called Club of Rome Report, issued a warning that, if the present growth trend in world population, industrialization, pollution, food production and resource depletion continue unchanged, the limits to growth on this planet will be reached sometime within the next one hundred years. [3]

The universal or global nature of the crisis lies not only in the fact that it affected practically all parts of the world, due to the increasingly integrated and global character of the world economy. Nor was the crisis global simply in the sense of the all-encompassing interconnectedness of the problems. It was global, first and foremost, in that the problems faced were of such a nature that, while they may be experienced locally, they could only be dealt with by concerted global action across the borders of nation-states, traditionally the basic units of political action.

Several attempts were made during the 1970s to arrive at a comprehensive statement of the world's problems. The Report of the Club of Rome, mentioned above, may have received the most attention, but there were also other earnest attempts at a comprehensive inventory made by: the International Institute of Applied Systems Analysis, the World Model Institute, the Russian Institute of System Studies, and the Batelle Institute, among others. But no other listing of global problems approaches the comprehensiveness of Aurelio Peccei's *The Human Quality* (1979).[4] That list includes:

- uncontrolled human proliferation

---

[3] D.H. Meadows, *The limits to Growth: the Report of the Club of Rome* (1972).

[4] Aurelio Peccei, *The Human Quality* (1979).

- chaos and divisions in society
- social injustice
- hunger and malnutrition
- widespread poverty
- the mania for growth
- inflation
- energy crisis
- international trade and monetary disruptions
- protectionism
- illiteracy and anachronistic education
- youth rebellion
- alienation
- uncontrolled urban spread and decay
- crime and drugs
- violence and brutality
- torture and terrorism
- disregard for law and order
- nuclear folly
- sclerosis and inadequacy of institutions
- corruption
- bureaucratization
- degradation of environment

- decline of moral values

- loss of faith

- sense of instability

- lack of understanding of the above problems and their interrelationship.

2. The Crisis of Values and International Efforts

As the sense of uncertainty and crisis deepened, it became increasingly clear that the ideas, assumptions and institutions on which modern society had been founded were no longer adequate to deal with many of the problems facing humanity. The crisis was increasingly seen as a crisis of ideas, beliefs and values that had been the foundation of the modern society, in the face of new historical realities engendered by the accelerating process of globalization. Nation-states, which had been the cornerstones of modern political development in the West since the middle of the 17th century, were being pulled apart by the contradictory forces of economic globalization and ethnic fragmentation. Since Westphalia, the nation-state had come to be seen as the only valid form of political-social organization. It was now woefully inadequate to deal with the new wave of global, transboundary problems. The model of political authority that had been at the basis of modern society was based on the supremacy of nation-states and national interests, and not on the idea of global responsibility and governance.

The full global dimension of the developing crisis was beginning to be appreciated by the international community throughout the 1970s and 1980s. The United Nations established over a period of seven years three independent commissions to report on different aspects of what was coming to be recognized as a common crisis. The Independent Commission on International Development Issues (known as the Brandt Commission) was established in 1977. In 1980, the Independent Commission on Disarmament and Security Issues (the Palme Commission) was constituted, while the Brundtland Commission on Environment and Development came into being in 1984.

The 1990s saw a remarkable series of world conferences convened by the United Nations, all addressing problems of a global magnitude. It was acknowledged that the solution of these problems exceeds the capacities of individual Member States, and depends upon a concerted international effort. The eight conferences were:

- 1990: World Summit for Children

- 1992: UN Conference on Environment and Development

- 1993: World Conference on Human Rights

- 1994: International Conference on Population and Development

- 1995: World Summit for Social Development

- 1995: Fourth World Conference on Women

- 1996: Second UN Conference on Human Settlement (Habitat II)[5]

The international community convened other major

---

[5] *The World Conferences: Developing Priorities for the 21st Century*(UN Briefing Paper, Department of Public Information, United Nations, NY, 1997).

conferences to address some of the most pressing problems facing the world today. They included:

- 1994: UN Global Conference on the Sustainable Development of Small Island Developing States

- 1994: International Conference on Natural Disaster Reduction

- 1995: 9th UN Congress on the Prevention of Crime and the Treatment of Offenders

- 1996: 9th UN Conference on Trade and Development (UNCTAD IX)

All of the conferences focused on issues of global well-being and sought to identify ways to link the problems people face at the community level with policies and actions at the international level. They were predicated on the recognition that the world is facing problems that cannot be resolved with action only at the national level.

The conferences together formed a cohesive series of meetings dealing with interrelated issues such as environmental protection, the well-being of children, human rights and the rights of women, population, unemployment, crime, trade, food security and human settlement.

While these conferences built on common ground created over decades by previous world conferences and conventions, there was an increasing demand for an integrated, interrelated and coherent implementation of their outcomes along a common framework. The conferences reflect the increasing acceptance of shared values, shared goals and the strategies to achieve them. The call for a "common framework" for the various initiatives echoed in the conferences reflects the growing convergence of views that democracy, development, and respect for human rights and fundamental freedoms are all interdependent and mutually reinforcing.

Thus, along with producing action plans and exploring the possibilities of expanding normative guidelines, these conferences played a role in the emergence of global principles such as human-centered development, the priority of poverty eradication, and a concept of justice expressed as the inseparability of civil and political from economic and social rights.

The clearest example is Agenda 21, the Rio Declaration on Environment and Development, which produced not only concrete conventions on climate change and biodiversity, but principles to guide international action on the environment:

Agenda 21 Principles

- *Human beings are at the center of concerns for sustainable development. They are entitled to a healthy and productive life in harmony with nature.*

- *Scientific uncertainty should not delay measures to prevent environmental degradation where there are threats of serious or irreversible damage.*

- *States have a sovereign right to exploit their own resources but not to cause damage to the environment of other States.*

- *Eradicating poverty and reducing disparities in worldwide standards of living are "indispensable" for sustainable development.*

- *Full participation of women is essential for achieving sustainable development.* [6]

Developed countries acknowledge the responsibility that they bear in the international pursuit of sustainable development in view of the pressures their societies place on the global environment and of the technologies and financial resources they command.

Common themes reappear in the final documents of all these meetings. The 1990 Children's Summit produced a document whose principles are clearly indicated in its title: World Declaration and Plan of Action on the Survival, Protection and Development of Children. The 1993 Vienna Declaration and Programme of Action emphasized a holistic approach linking development, democracy and human rights. The Population Conference likewise stressed that poverty reduction, environmental protection and the promotion of gender equality work as "mutually reinforcing" factors to slow population growth. The Social Summit's Copenhagen Declaration united social, economic, political and cultural concerns in its "ten commitments" to enhance quality of life, transcending cultural differences. The Beijing Women's Conference addressed 12 areas of concern, in which women are fairly systematically excluded from enjoying their nationally and internationally recognized rights and freedoms. The Habitat and Food Conferences focused attention on two of the most basic components of human well-being.

At the same time, a reappraisal of the factors that augment the quality of life began to call into question the link between

---

[6] *Ibid.* p.24.

simple development and well-being. Dramatic urban growth, mass unemployment, social disintegration, and historically unprecedented polarities of wealth and poverty are consequences of development. According to studies such as UNICEF's *Giving Children a Future: The World Summit for Children* (1990) and *State of the World's Children* reports, as well as the 1996 report of the Independent Commission on Population and Quality of Life, economic growth is not necessarily associated with improvement in quality of life. For benefits to be realized, allocation and distribution of resources require some ethical orientation in the light of near universally shared aims and values.[7]

3. The Western Synthesis

The symptoms of uncertainty and crisis that mark this *fin-de-siècle* are, in an important sense, a reflection of the inability of nation-states to deal effectively with the new historical situation. But one could argue that even this inability reflects a crisis in the synthesis of ideas and values that had taken the West several centuries to develop. Based on the ideas of individualism, rationalism, scientism and teleology of progress, the Western synthesis provided a point of reference as societies endeavored to industrialize and modernize. The synthesis had such a preeminence in the minds and affairs of men that nations and societies were practically unanimous in accepting Westernization as the only means of ensuring a viable future. Under the banner of modernization, they abandoned customary truths, values and ways of life, and accepted their degree of Westernization as their measure of progress or regress.

---

[7] *Caring for the Future*, Report of the Independent Commission on Population and Quality of Life (Oxford University Press, 1996).

Today the Western synthesis of ideas and values seems no longer able to offer a sure guide to human survival and flourishing. After the demise of socialism and gradual retreat of the welfare state, the mixed economy of the Keynesian and Asian-values provenience, there does seem to be a certain triumphalism on the part of the advocates of the neo-liberal economic model in today's globalizing economy. They seem, however, unable to deal with the growing impoverishment of much of the South, as well as with phenomena of mass unemployment and growing pauperization of a significant segment of the population in the North.

Many countries in the Third World, having won independence from their former colonial powers, pursued industrialization. In need of the capital and the know-how, they were heavily dependent on the developed world. Today the largest portion of the budgets of many of these countries goes toward servicing their loans, some paying up to 70% of their GNP for this purpose. Nearly one third of the population in developing countries live in absolute poverty, while 100 million children are homeless street-dwellers. [8] Even in the richer countries more than 100 million people live in poverty, and the ranks of the poor are growing. [9]

It is all too clear that the benefits of globalization do not extend to all countries or social groups. Indeed, the dramatic extremes of wealth and poverty born of globalization menace both democracy and social stability in various regions. For many it signifies a race to the bottom, not only in wages but in standards of environmental regulation and social legislation.

---

[8] UNRISD, States of Disarray: The Social Effects of Globalization (London, 1995).

[9] As reported in the International Herald Trubune, Sept. 10, 1998, quoting the Annual Report of UNDP.

And by empowering economic entities over political ones, it has given rise to historically unprecedented heights of regional financial instability. This global state of affairs casts doubt on the once dominant and pervasive cultural model that guided its development.

II. The Search for Common Values: Tentative Steps

It is against this backdrop of fragmentation and uncertainty for human well-being that the search for common ethical values and principles must be seen. Efforts began to crystallize in the 1990s to frame possible solutions to the global problems in comprehensive, ethical terms. Among international organizations, commissions, academic, religious and political institutions, as well as among individual thinkers and advocates, we are witnessing a number of vigorous attempts to arrive at new syntheses of ideas and values that would be acceptable across cultures and societies and relevant to the tasks of human survival and flourishing. We are also witnessing an almost explosive emergence of the so-called one-issue NGOs; these organizations are often expressions of a new value awareness emerging from a situation of cultural disarray and political disempowerment of national governments and other public instances.

It must not be forgotten, however, that the new concern with values also has its negative side: the revival of chauvinisms, the proliferation of sometimes hazardous new religious movements, and the growing strength of various forms of fundamentalism. Whether negative or positive, the phenomenon of value awareness is intimately connected with the realization that the global problems that render our traditional values, ideas and institutions impotent must be dealt with in a creative and novel way. It represents the realization that an important, if not the most important, part of such an effort must be concentrated on forging a new cultural synthesis of ideas and values necessary to deal with the problems of human survival and flourishing in an age of globalization.

1. International Commissions

In recent years, a number of studies have drawn particular attention to the need to articulate universal norms, values or principles that could serve as the basis for peaceful and productive interaction among nations and societies, prevention of conflicts and crises, and collective efforts toward peace and prosperity.

a) Our Global Neighborhood

Our Global Neighborhood, the report of the Commission on Global Governance, came out strongly in 1995 for a "global civic ethic"[10] as the foundation for cooperation among different societies and cultures facing common global problems. Such a global ethics comprises a common moral minimum of core values shared by all cultures and religious traditions, and a set of rights and responsibilities constituting a "civic code" based on these core values. These values include: respect for life, liberty, justice and equity, mutual respect, caring and integrity. They are seen as derived in one way or another from the principle of reciprocity known as the Golden Rule — that people should treat others as they would themselves wish to be treated.

The report then presents a list of rights and responsibilities based on these core values and representing the minimum basis for progress in building a global civil society. The rights

---

[10] *Our Global Neighborhood,* The Commission on Global Governance (Oxford, 1995), p.55.

include: the rights to a secure life, equitable treatment, an opportunity to earn a fair living, participation in governance at all levels, equal access to information and, finally, equal access to the global commons. The responsibilities, on the other hand, include: to consider the impact of our actions on others, to promote equity, including gender equity, to protect the interests of future generations, to safeguard the global commons, to preserve humanity's cultural and intellectual heritage, to be active participants in governance and to work to eliminate corruption.

b) Our Creative Diversity

Also in 1995, the World Commission on Culture and Development, chaired by Javier Pérez de Cuellar, former Secretary-General of the United Nations, published its report *Our Creative Diversity*.[11] The report makes a plea for a "global ethics", a core of shared ethical values and principles, that would provide the minimum moral guidance the world needs in its efforts to deal with global issues. Conflicts can be limited within bounds and cooperation between different peoples facilitated if people can see themselves as being bound and motivated by shared commitments. Since all societies need a basis of moral principles for their self-regulation, social order and international relations, there is no reason why ethics should stop at national borders.

The Commission maintains that global ethics could provide the minimum requirements any government and people should meet, while leaving a scope for political creativity, social imagination and cultural pluralism. Such an ethics could be composed of: 1) human rights and responsibilities; 2)

---

[11] *Our Creative Diversity*, The World Commission on Culture and Development (UNESCO. 1995).

democracy and the elements of civil society, such as free, fair and regular elections, freedom of press and information, and the freedom of association ; 3) protection of minority rights ; 4) commitment to peaceful conflict resolution and fair negotiation ; and 5) equity within and between generations.

2. Religious, Political and Cultural Institutions

a) The Parliament of the World's Religions

In 1993, representatives of more than 120 religions of the world, meeting for the first time in one hundred years in the Parliament of the World's Religions in Chicago, adopted a Declaration towards a Global Ethic. [12] The text of this Declaration was drafted by Dr. Hans Küng, the German Catholic theologian who has for a number of years been at the forefront of the effort to forge a global ethics acceptable to all religions and adequate to deal with the issues arising from a fundamental crisis in global economy, ecology and politics. The starting point of the Declaration is the recognition that there exists within religious teachings of the world a consensus that speaks directly to current global problems. This consensus serves as the basis of a global ethics — a minimal, fundamental consensus concerning binding values, irrevocable standards and fundamental moral attitudes.

The 1993 Declaration confirms the existence of two principles which represent a "fundamental demand" of all religious and ethical traditions, namely, that every human being must be treated humanely, and what you do not wish done to

---

[12] Parliament of the World's Religions/Kuschel, *A Global Ethic: The Declaration of the Parliament of the World's Religions* (Chicago: Continuum Publishing Group, 1994).

yourself, do not do to others. Further, these principles are seen to give rise to broad moral guidelines which are found in most religions of the world. They are: 1) a commitment to a culture of non-violence and respect for life ; 2) a commitment to a culture of solidarity and a just economic order ; 3) a commitment to a culture of tolerance and a life of truthfulness ; and, finally, 4) a commitment to a culture of equal rights and partnership between men and women.

b) The InterAction Council

In 1997, some thirty former heads of state and government who constitute the InterAction Council submitted a draft of a "Universal Declaration of Human Responsibilities" to all heads of state and government and to the United Nations and UNESCO. They did so, wrote Helmut Schmidt, who has been the moving force behind the Declaration, "in a hope that the United Nations will adopt our proposed declaration, or at least its spirit, on the 50th Anniversary of the 1948 Human Rights Declaration". [13]

The Declaration of Responsibilities, drafted by Dr. Küng and a group of experts in a series of discussions over a period of two years, consists of a preamble and 19 articles that are ordered under 5 different headings. These headings are: fundamental principles of humanity (4 articles), non-violence and respect for life (3 articles), justice and solidarity (4 articles), truthfulness and tolerance (4 articles), mutual respect and partnership (3 articles) and a conclusion. It is clear that the structure and content of the Declaration are essentially those of the 1993 Declaration adopted by the Parliament of World's Religions, expressed now however in quasi-legalistic format

---

[13] Helmut Schmidt, letter accompanying *"A Declaration of Human Responsibilities, Proposed by the InterAction Council"*, Sept. 3, 1997.

and language befitting its occasion and sponsorship.

The ethical values and standards identified in the proposed Declaration of Responsibilities are seen to be necessary elements for the creation of a better social order and for the realization of human aspirations for progress. Based on the perception that "exclusive insistence on rights can lead to endless dispute and conflict", it seeks to balance freedom with responsibility, but also to reconcile ideologies, beliefs and political views, in apparent reference to the debate between Western proponents of human rights and proponents of the so-called "Asian values". The Declaration's provision on freedom of the press in Article 14, which emphasizes a special responsibility for accurate and truthful reporting, has been the subject of critical debate. Against the intention of the sponsors of the Declaration to supplement the Universal Declaration of Human Rights, some press associations have denounced it as "diluting" the 1948 Human Rights Declaration.

c) The Institute for Global Ethics

For Rushworth Kidder, the founder of the Institute for Global Ethics (USA), ethics is rapidly becoming as much a survival issue as the nuclear threat, environmental degradation, the population crisis, the gap between haves and have-nots and the need for education reform. In *Shared Values for a Troubled World*,[14] Kidder identifies a number of cross-cultural core values: love, truthfulness, fairness, freedom, unity, tolerance, responsibility and respect for life.

The method used by Kidder is sometimes called "Delphic". He interviews a number of individuals of high moral influence

---

[14] Rushworth M. Kidder, *Shared Values for a Troubled World* (San Francisco, 1994).

and sensitivity on the question of what values or sets of values could be identified to form a global code of ethics that would help humanity to deal with the problems enumerated in the preceding paragraph. The interviewees include a Buddhist monk, a former president of Harvard, a Chinese author, an American philosopher, Mozambique's former first lady and a former Director-General of UNESCO. They form the source from which the above eight values are pulled together. Kidder considers them the principles which could contribute to meeting a pressing need for shared values, and from which we may build "downward" to the level of goals, plans and tactics.

d) The Third Millennium Project

A Declaration of Human Duties and Responsibilities was presented to UNESCO in April, 1999, by the Third Millennium Project of the City of Valencia, Spain, in cooperation with UNESCO and ADC Nouveau Millénaire, to commemorate the arrival of the year 2000. The document was drafted by a "high-level group" chaired by South African Justice Richard J. Goldstone and including Richard Falk, Bernard Kouchner, Ruud Lubbers, Joseph Rothblat and Wole Soyinka among others. The Declaration was the result of congresses hosted by the City of Valencia on "Human Responsibilities and Duties in the Third Millennium: Towards a Pax Planetaria" (January and April 1998) and "The Universal Declaration of Human Duties and Responsibilities" (December 1998).

The avowed aim of the Declaration of Human Duties and Responsibilities is to renew the resolve of the international community to rededicate itself to the implementation of human rights and responsibilities by making clear the relationship between rights, duties and responsibilities. Reaffirming the universal significance of the Universal Declaration of Human Rights and the related Covenants, the drafters of the Valencia

Declaration consider that the realization of rights and freedoms are dependent on the assumption of the political, moral, ethical and legal duties and responsibilities which are implicit in human rights and fundamental freedoms recognized by all relevant players in the global community, including states, intergovernmental and non-governmental organizations, the private sector and other representatives of civil society, communities, peoples and individuals. Hence the need for an explicit formulation of duties and responsibilities.

The Declaration consists of a preamble, twelve chapters and forty-one articles, spelling out in great detail the duties and responsibilities accruing to different players in different sectors of the international community. The twelve chapters of the Declaration are: general provisions (Articles 1-2); the right to life and human security (Articles 3-9); human security and an equitable international order (Articles 10-15); meaningful participation in public affairs (Article 16); freedom of opinion, expression, assembly, association and religion (Articles 17-20); the right to personal and physical integrity (Articles 21-25); equality (Articles 26-30); protection of minorities and indigenous peoples (Articles 31-32); rights of the child and the elderly (Articles 33-34); work quality of life and standard of living (Articles 35-36); education, arts and culture (Articles 37-38); and finally a right to a remedy (Articles 39-41).[15]

3. Global Common Values in Action

a) Business and Finance

In practice, sets of international ethical norms and

---

[15] Cf. *Declaration of Human Duties and Responsibilities: Background Documents* (Fundacion Valencia Tercer Milenio, Valencia, 1999).

principles are already operating and evolving in many sectors of society. In international business and financial institutions around the world, the Bretton Woods institutions including the IMF and the World Bank or the World Trade Organization set rules and regulations which the members of these organizations ignore only at their peril.

Multilateral agreements exist, covering services such as banking and insurance, and intellectual property rights. They bind national governments, limiting their domestic policy choices. The principles underlying these rules and regulations may be competition, profit, deregulation and transparency. The failure so far of OECD countries to reach an agreement on a Multilateral Agreement on Investment (MAI) is also an indication of the difficulty of all attempts to agree upon a globally valid set of codes of conduct, even limited in application to a particular sector.

b) International Governance Agencies

For further illustrations of global ethics in action today, one may point to the dominant value orientations of many international governance agencies which are global in their scope of activities, e.g., the United Nations and its agencies, such as UNESCO, UNICEF and WHO. The United Nations Charter and the Universal Declaration of Human Rights articulate their dominant values, endorsed by their signatories. There are also the so-called Third Sector organizations, representing "international civil society". Many of these NGOs advocate or implement particular values — such as Médecins-sans-frontières or Amnesty International. A recent study estimates that the non-profit organizations in just 22 countries are a $1.1 trillion sector, employing 19 million people.[16] Collectively considered, their key values include voluntarism, care and social justice.

c) Global Academic and Cultural Conventions

Academic, scientific and professional organizations, as well as the press, have sometimes precisely defined codes of ethics as they exchange knowledge and information on a worldwide basis across national frontiers. Their dominant values include truthfulness, right to intellectual property, free flow of information, and others which may from time to time come into conflict with national legislations. A similar situation exists in arts, sport and entertainment. Performances in these fields have been globalized by the mass media, and they are governed by agreed standards and practices, supported by a certain commonality in appreciation of aesthetic qualities. One should also add that globalization is strengthening the transnational dimension of crime. International mafias, drug cartels and terrorist organizations are among the first to take advantage of relaxation of border controls and advances in communication and transportation. Their operations across national frontiers are based on a set of implicit codes of behavior, the breach of which is bound to be met with due consequences.

III.Prospects

1.Toward the Ethics Charter of the 21st Century

How, then, do we proceed from here in our journey to arrive at an ethical statement that could serve as a universally

---

[16] UNDP Human Development Report, 1999, p.36.

acceptable guideline as humanity struggles to deal with the tasks of survival and flourishing in the 21st century ? The outer sign posts of such a statement have been clearly posited. It is to be a maximalist document that would contain ethical values and principles adequate and relevant to the myriad of problems facing humanity in the coming century, to be ascertained by empirical as well as by reflective methods. Such a document must also be acceptable universally, although universality must not be exclusive, but inclusive in that it must be capable of accommodating cultural diversity that characterizes the world today. Furthermore, it must be an ethical document of higher axiological order than the human rights charter, showing how the particular rights and responsibilities enshrined in it could be derived from the values and principles contained in the document.

A necessary first step is to make an inventory of ethical values and principles which have been proposed in many declarations and studies, both private and public, national and international, and religious and secular, designed to deal with a certain set of problems facing humanity. Five different categories of such documents are scouted for this purpose :

- values and principles proposed in intergovernmental documents ;

- values and principles advocated in the reports of international commissions and declarations of international conferences ;

- values and principles identified in non-governmental projects and surveys ;

- values and principles put forth by individuals, mainly by participants in the meetings organized in connection with the Universal Ethics Project;

- values and principles proposed by different religious traditions of the world.

Once the values and principles are thus identified, they will be set in relation to the problems for which they are intended to be the solution. It is clear, however, that the list of problems facing humanity which requires approaches through common universal values can vary greatly according to the level of generality and concreteness at which the problems are identified and described. It can also vary according to the vantage point from which the authors of the documents approach the problems. The participants of the first meeting in Paris, for instance, identified eight such problems, while Aurelio Peccei's list encompasses twenty-seven. Indeed, the *Encyclopedia of World Problems and Human Potential* [17] claims to have identified some 12,203 world problems put forth in international journals and in the documents of some 20,000 international non-profit organizations. In order to circumvent the difficulty inherent in this profusion of problem lists, we have found it useful to make an inventory of problems and issues facing humanity, the solution to which can only be found in the realm of ethical values and principles.

What, then, are the basic issues and problems around which the ethical values and principles could be organized ? The following is one among many such proposals, containing several clusters of issues and problems. First, there is the problem of fundamental readjustment of the human relationship to nature. The fundamental dynamic at work here is one of accommodating unlimited human needs and desires to

---

[17] *Encyclopedia of World Problems and Human Potential*, Vol. I (Union of International Associations, Munich, K.G. Saur, 1994), p.60.

a limited planetary ecosystem. Our relationship to nature must enable us to manage our economy while sustaining the complexity and stability of nature to sustain our economy. The task ahead is not simply to control nature but to control ourselves as well, so that the economy can fit within the natural ecology. The way we face this challenge is related to the way we see the human person : as a being separate from nature, or as one species among others embedded in the intricate web of natural processes that contains and sustains all forms of life.

The first cluster of issues leads naturally to a second : the conception of what constitutes human happiness or, to put it in another way, of what constitutes the meaning of life, or human fulfillment. Our views regarding what ultimately constitutes the meaning of life are bound to influence the priorities we assign to values and thus the way we behave, both in relation to ourselves and others. An attitude that sees human happiness in the accumulation of material wealth may be contrasted with a holistic perspective, which would enable us to balance and coordinate satisfaction among different dimensions of human existence: between "inner" satisfaction and satisfaction of the material kind.

Such a revision is intimately connected with the issue of the relationship between the individual and the community in which he has his existential root. The basic problem is the role we assign to individual freedom and creativity on the one hand, and the need for the stability and order of the community, on the other, without which no meaningful human existence is possible. The aggressive, individualistic ethics that formed the backbone of modern industrial civilization may require some revision and tempering by greater concern for the human good. The problem of the individual in his relationship to the community is a particularly difficult one, since a universal ethics worthy of the name must be one that has a place of honor for individuals and their creativity.

The issue of individualism is intimately connected with the problem of justice, both among individuals at national levels and among nations at international levels. Injustice, at national as well as international levels, is the most important source of disruption in the fabric of society, as well as of conflict among nations. We see at play the tensions between equality and freedom, between the good of one individual or group and another, and between rights and responsibilities. Many conceptions of justice in social organization have been tried : paternalism, colonialism, utilitarianism, capitalism, socialism and now market liberalism. They have all been found to be wanting in fundamental respects, some more than others. Universal ethics must be able to point a way that goes beyond any or all of these.

2. The Task Ahead

The task, then, is how to interrelate the problems and needs of humanity thus identified and the values and principles thus scouted into a persuasive and coherent whole which can serve as the guide for humanity in its tasks of survival and flourishing. It is clear that such a document does not exhaust itself in a simple decretal listing or inventorying of the ascertained values and principles. It must be capable of demonstrating the relationship among these values and principles in such a way that the relationship of foundation and derivation is made clear. Further, since the aim is to forge an ethical statement that is acceptable to all societies and cultures built on different perceptions and aspirations, it must be capable of accommodating the challenge of cultural diversity and polarities of values and principles. Such diversity and polarity reflect not only the living dilemma of action in terms of the values which give rise to it; it reflects the real source of conflict among cultures and societies. The approach of integrating diversity within each principle, rather than offering a hasty compromise, enables the participants in the ethical dialogue to sense the dimensions of the conflict and the space within which a consensus can be forged. The document must therefore be capable of making clear a dynamic relationship, a relationship of creative tension, among conflicting but not irreconcilable values such that a common vision can emerge in an open-ended, evolutionary process of dialogue and mutual learning.

What is offered in the following pages, A Common Framework for the Ethics of the 21st Century, is a document which goes a long way toward meeting the above requirements. It would however be foolhardy to expect that it will meet with the unanimous consent of the international community. At best, it will be the beginning and starting point of a long and arduous evolutionary process of intercultural debate and consensus-building. It is intended to serve as the framework within which a dialogue of humankind, a conversation of humankind, could take place, so that a common ethical vision can emerge out of this process of dialogue and mutual learning.

COMMON FRAMEWORK FOR ETHICS OF THE 21ST CENTURY

Preamble

Humanity stands at this century's end in a situation of extraordinary challenge and openness. Scientific and technological advances are creating new opportunities on a scale previously unimagined, even as they threaten to destroy the very foundation of human life. The forces of a globalizing economy are creating great wealth for humanity, even as they widen the gap between the haves and have-nots within and among societies and nations. Increasing global interdependence gives rise to ever more complex transboundary questions defying traditional solutions.

Ideas and institutions, values and practices that served humanity so well in its endeavour to industrialize and modernize are increasingly called into question. Individualism, rationalism, scientism and teleology of progress, which had been the driving forces of the modern industrial civilization, seem now to be working at cross purposes with the tasks of human survival and flourishing as societies and nations attempt to come to terms with the new historical realities. Yet, no culture is possible without agreement on a foundation of common values and ideas to guide the tasks of governance.

Global problems require global values. Such was the view shared by an impressive series of intergovernmental conferences organized by the United Nations, reports of international commissions, advocacies of academic, political and religious institutions, as well as the works of concerned individual thinkers around the world throughout the closing decade of the 20th century. It is clear that peaceful and productive cooperation among different peoples can be facilitated if they can see themselves as being bound and motivated by a shared commitment to a basis of ethical values and principles.

These are the impetus behind the present articulation of ethical values and principles viable and needed across cultures and societies. Its task is to identify and forge ethical values and principles into a coherent and dynamic whole adequate to deal with the problems facing humanity. The process of identification scouts certain views of the common good that are lived and practiced in daily life across cultures. The process of forging an ethical common ground is based on the global problems which humanity faces in common.

The universality of the present ethical articulation is then founded on the universality of the global problems it addresses. The task is both enriched and challenged by the cultural pluralism that characterizes contemporary societies. It allies itself with an inclusive notion of universality that is capable of accommodating the diversity of perceptions and aspirations of different cultures. Such a conception is based on two concrete facts: the commonality of ethical practice in the daily life of different cultures, and the commonality of the tasks which humanity faces.

Formulated in response to the global problems, the four sections represent those clusters of ethical values and principles which together would be adequate to meet the challenge. The four sections each strike a balance: sustainability for the earth, human fulfillment in the free exercise of both rights and responsibilities, complementarity between the individual and the community, and peace through justice.

Each principle within each section reflects the range of

positions afforded by the diversity and even polarity of values and principles, encompassing not only a lived dilemma of action but also a possible source of conflicts among cultures and societies, religions and world-views. In so doing, it also makes clear a dynamic relationship, a relationship of creative interaction among the conflicting but by no means irreconcilable values. Each principle allows us to see that the ideal terminus of such a dynamic relationship is a reflective equilibrium, optimally suited to deal with the problems at hand.

Different human communities, like individuals, share many ethical values. Above all, we share the common goal of survival and prospering. Today we are facing self-annihilation from problems which lie beyond the scope of law, and beyond the power of any individual person or nation to remedy. The scope of our ethical practice can no longer stop at the edge of our family, our society, or our nation. Hope lies in action in accordance with a shared ethics.

Here, then, is a common ethical framework within which all cultures, societies and individuals are invited to deliberate on the tasks of survival and flourishing. It invites all stakeholders in the ethics of the 21st century to take their respective positions. It is a framework for a conversation of humankind, the beginning of a long arduous evolutionary process in which the commonality of the problems facing humanity, in spite of differences which separate, will lead to a common ethical vision. It is a framework for a process that must be nurtured in an open-ended way through dialogue, mutual learning and above all, good will.

I. Relationship to Nature

1. The view of nature as accessible through causal-mechanistic law has enabled humanity to control nature and

provide for itself the good life on earth. The same view has also contributed to destruction of the natural environment and alienation of human beings. We must therefore seek a balance such that we may maintain a sustainable harmonious relationship between the human species and nature.

2. As nature is a finite quantity, we must learn to manage the economy to sustain the complexity and stability of nature while at the same time to manage nature so as to sustain our economy. As our desires are insatiable, we must learn to accommodate our desires to the limits nature sets, not to push the limits of nature beyond its capacity for regeneration.

3. Humanity needs to develop economically and technologically in order to deal with the problem of poverty in which a great majority of human beings still live. Continuation of economic development at the present rate endangers the rights of future generations to life and a healthy environment. We must therefore learn to balance short-term thinking and immediate gratification with long-term thinking for future generations by shifting the balance towards quality rather than quantity.

4. Consumption contributes to human well-being when it enlarges the capabilities and enriches the lives of the people. Consumption, when excessive, undermines the resource base and exacerbates inequalities. Consumption therefore must be such as to ensure basic needs for all, without compromising the well-being of others and without mortgaging the choices of future generations.

II. Human Fulfillment

1. Every person is unique in his or her individuality. He or she is at the same time embedded in a living tradition in which the ideas of a common good are transmitted. Thus meaningful

life entails an openness and dialogue with the cultural space that surrounds every individual.

2. Truthfulness promotes trust. Without trust, the foundation of relations among human beings and the possibility of a moral society are threatened. Truth-telling therefore is the fundamental presupposition of an ethical life.

3. Preponderance of emotion impairs our ability to think clearly about the possibilities and consequences of choice. Yet, exclusive emphasis on reason tends to make humans cold and calculating. Thus, thinking and feeling should be seen as complements, mutually enriching each other.

4. The life of individual satisfaction is ultimately shallow and narcissistic. The life of transcendent goals often slips into fanaticism and denial of life. Mindful of the deeper structure of our life, we must cultivate an active moral intuition entailing a connection to the idea of the good.

5. Since a human person is possessed of both mind and body, requiring both spiritual and material fulfillment, pursuit of wealth must be tempered by the cultivation of the mind. Outer satisfactions of a material kind should be enhanced by the inner satisfaction of the mind and spirit, and vice versa.

III. Individual and Community

1. Everyone should be treated with respect, embodying a set of rights which an individual possesses as an attribute of his or her dignity as a human being. At the same time he or she must be recognized as the center of relationships, encompassing family, society, nation and humanity of which he or she is a part. Every individual must therefore be seen as the locus of both rights and responsibilities.

2. While the claims of different groups to live according to

their authentic values should be respected, emphasis on cultural identity should not be self-centered and exclusivistic. Self-centeredness can only be overcome by willingness for dialogue and mutual learning.

3. Without order, anarchy prevails; without autonomy communities turn into authoritarian states. We must therefore strive for an equilibrium between individual rights and the concern for the common good such that individual rights and respect for the common good enhance each other.

4. We must give help to people and communities in need. Prolonged reliance on help from others weakens creativity and initiative. Help must therefore be rendered in such a way as to promote the creativity and initiative of those being helped.

5. Dialogue alone is incapable of solving the problems facing humanity. Yet, action without dialogue often leads to unintended aggression. Recognizing that dialogue is essential to harmonious co-existence, we must learn to act in such a way that dialogue accompanies every action.

IV. Justice

1. While every person should be treated equally, it is also necessary that everyone should be free to develop his or her potentialities to the fullest. We must therefore learn to balance claims of equality and claims of freedom such that every individual is able to realize his or her potentialities to the fullest extent possible, compatible with similar freedoms for others.

2. Globalization holds great potential to enhance human welfare. It also widens the gap between rich and poor, among individuals, groups and nations. It must therefore be managed to the advantage of weaker nations, disadvantaged groups and

individuals.

3. In order to maintain a society in which democracy and human rights are respected, the livelihood of the people must be sustained. It should be an explicit policy objective to ensure that all have enough to eat, adequate housing and decent employment, that no child goes without education, that no human being is denied access to health care, safe water and basic sanitation. We must live simply in order that others may simply live.

4. In defense against aggression and intolerance, the use of force may become necessary. Yet force may create counter violence. We must therefore aim at an effective rule of law, including at the international level.

5. Too much legislation numbs the sense of individual responsibility. Too little legislation leads to anarchy and disorder. Legislation is best when it is conducive to promotion of individual responsibility.

DIALOGUE AMONG CIVILIZATIONS AT THE UNITED NATIONS: THE COMING AGE OF GLOBAL SOLIDARITY

Abdelkader Abbadi, Ph.D.

Dr. Abdelkader Abbadi was born in Morocco. He is a graduate of the University of California and holds a Ph.D. in Political Science and International Economic Relations. Dr. Abbadi worked for the United Nations in the Department of Political Affairs for over thirty years and served in several senior positions, including Chief of the Asia Division, Deputy Director of the Security Council Affairs Division, and Director of Africa Division. He is presently a Senior Diplomatic Correspondent for the Diplomatic World Observer at the United Nations in New York. Previous to that, Dr. Abbadi also wrote for the Paris based *Jeune Afrique* weekly magazine.

"...Modern science affirms what ancient faith has always taught: the most important fact of life is our common humanity."

President Bill Clinton

State of the Union address to Congress,

January 27, 2000

INTRODUCTION

In his New Year's message to his Holiness Pope John Paul II on the occasion of the advent of the New Millennium, the President of the Islamic Republic of Iran, Seyyed Mohammad Khatami said:

Humanity at the threshold of the 21st century is more than ever in need of peace, freedom, justice, and security. Overcoming of bloody and sad events of the 20th century is only possible through fundamental changes in thinking and political foundations, and changing the framework of existing international relations and replacing them with new concepts such as dialogue among civilizations and cultures...I hope by adherence to the principles of co-existence (he left out the traditional adjective 'peaceful'), mutual respect, dialogue among civilizations, cultures and religions, we will witness strengthening of principles of peace, based on justice, friendship, and mutual respect for all human beings.[1]

Some five years earlier, on October 5, 1995, His Holiness John Paul II concluded his address to the Fiftieth Commemorative Session of the General Assembly of the United Nations by declaring:

We have within us the capacities for wisdom and virtue. With these gifts, and the help of God's grace, we can build in the next century and the next millennium a civilization

---

[1] President Seyyed Mohammad Khatami: Message to His Holiness Pope John Paul II on the occasion of the year 2000.

worthy of the human person, a true culture of freedom. We can and must do so! And in doing so, we shall see that the tears of this century have prepared the ground for a new springtime of the human spirit.[2]

The "Dialogue among Civilizations" has commenced at the United Nations. The General Assembly at its Fifty-third session, fall of 1998, adopted resolution 53/22, through which it expressed its firm determination to facilitate and promote dialogue among civilizations and decided to proclaim the year 2001 as the United Nations Year of that dialogue.

A major objective of this article consists in the examination of the extent to which the current discussions on the subject at the United Nations and the trends to which they are giving rise reflect the depth of thinking of these two leaders, Mohammad Khatami and Pope John Paul II.

A NEW VISION FOR A NEW CENTURY

The advent of the new millennium has given birth to hopes in the international community that the new century will usher in a period that would inaugurate a more peaceful and more productive stage in human history and would contribute to humankind's elevation to a higher level of material and spiritual progress. Unprecedented celebrations took place worldwide to welcome this event and several programs and demonstrations are planned to that effect. Pope John Paul II proclaimed the year 2000 a Jubilee Year. Musicians are actively working on a new symphony for the new times. The United Nations and the NGO community will be holding

---

[2] His Holiness John Paul II: address to the Fiftieth Session of the General Assembly of the United Nations, 5 October 1997.

parallel meetings to celebrate new activities for the new century. The UN General Assembly, as seen above, has proclaimed 2001 as the year of Dialogue among Civilizations to promote harmony, understanding, and peace, and to prevent what Samuel Huntington foresaw as the coming "clash of civilizations."[3] It is obvious however, that in a new age characterized by rapid, profound scientific and technological changes, by an apparent decline of values, by confusion and loss of direction, what is most essentially needed is creative thinking; not a thinking de-coupled from reality, but one that is based on it; not just the reality of today, but also the new, emerging reality.

Mohammad Khatami and Pope John II appear to be the promoters of this reality of tomorrow. What they foresee for the new millennium are profound transformations with far-reaching implications for humankind and its institutions. The first speaks of "fundamental changes in thinking and political foundations"; the second, of "a civilization worthy of the human person, a true culture of peace." Scientists today announce the "convergence" of computers, telephones, television, agriculture and lasers. But they also talk about another long-term, higher level of convergence—the "meta-convergence" of technology and culture, including religion, epistemology, and the rest of intellectual life. This last convergence brings with it new ideas, new beliefs, new ways of thinking, new values, and new lifestyles. Alvin and Heidi Toffler observed: "Technologies may converge with one another, but they also converge with elements of society and culture, in ways that produce not simply profit for this or that company, or the restructuring of industries and economies, but,

---

[3] Samuel P. Huntington, The Clash of Civilizations and the Remaking of World Order, Simon & Schuster, 1997.

over time, the restructuring and convergence of whole civilizations. All this is heading our way. Welcome to the 21st century!"[4] Michael Gorbachev spoke about "new civilization" and our "epoch making" stage in man's history. Bill Gates, Chairman of Microsoft, in the *Road Ahead*, says that "we are watching something historic happen, and it will affect the world seismically." Bill Gates is thrilled by "squinting into the future and catching that first revealing hint of revolutionary possibilities." He feels incredibly lucky "to be playing a part in the beginning of an epochal change."[5]

Technology, of course, was not born today, and with each invention, whether it was the railroad locomotive, the telephone, the radio, the TV, or the fax, we were told that the world was getting smaller. Then came the most global development of all, the majestic internet. But during all this time, the world has not liberated itself from violence. The twentieth century has been described as the most violent century ever known to humankind. And in the words of Tom Wolfe, "what have the breathtaking advances in communications technology done for the human mind?"[6] That is why the Pope has spoken so eloquently about the tears of this century preparing the ground for "a new springtime of the human spirit".

Others have also observed that technology is not an end in itself, but that it should be put at the service of humankind.

---

[4] Alvin & Heidi Toffler, "Eruptions from the Future – the next 50 years will raise enormous ethical questions", Forbes ASAP, October 4, 1999, pp185-186.

[5] Tom Wolfe: "Digibabble, Fairy Dust, and the Human Anthill", in Forbes ASAP op. cited.

[6] Tom Wolfe: op. cit.

Already in the sixteenth century, French writer François Rabelais warned that "science sans conscience n'est que ruine de l'âme." In modern times, Albert Einstein often said that "science without religion is lame, religion without science is blind."

Everywhere one looks today, there seems to be a confluence of various branches of knowledge. The study of modern genetics raises moral and ethical questions. A dialogue between ethics and the natural sciences has already begun. Today, we talk about the preservation of nature, the necessity of a clean environment, and of the responsibility of corporations in investments. Scientists are now paying close attention to people's yearning for a spiritual and meaningful life.

At the United Nations, a dialogue has begun among a diversity of civilizations. Will they achieve convergence on the burning issues of our times, such as peace, the elimination of poverty, and social and economic progress for all? Can they transcend their narrow interests, and begin to establish the foundations of a true cooperation to tackle these issues?

DIALOGUE AMONG CIVILIZATIONS

President Seyyed Mohammad Khatami launched the idea of dialogue among civilizations on 21 September 1998, when he addressed the Fifty-third session of the General Assembly. The thrust of his statement consisted in calling "for a dialogue among civilizations and cultures instead of a clash between them," in the hope that justice and liberty would prevail. Echoing somewhat the optimistic vision formulated by Pope John Paul II referred to earlier, President Khatami declared:

From this rostrum and the pulpit of the United Nations, I announce that humanity, despite all calamities and hardships, is heading towards emancipation and liberty. This is the unalterable divine providence and human destiny. The malice and depravity of no individual can ever violate divine providence and the course of history.[7]

When the representative of Iran introduced the resolution on the subject to the Fifty-fourth session of the General Assembly on 10 December 1999, he indicated that dialogue among civilizations could potentially take mere tolerance of diversity a few steps further, raising the level of discourse to higher planes of caring, genuine cooperation and constructive engagement.[8] The dialogue, he pursued, would foster mutual respect for and understanding of differences among peoples. At the same meeting, the representative of Finland, speaking on behalf of the European Union, stated that dialogue among civilizations was an excellent way to promote pluralism and tolerance, as well as to promote civil society's participation in the process of governance. Other speakers at the same meeting mentioned human rights, tolerance and cultural cooperation. One of them stated that dialogue among civilizations should aim at overcoming differences of opinion among peoples.[9]

In its original resolution, [10] the Assembly invited governments, the United Nations, and other relevant international and non-governmental organizations to plan and

---

[7] Seyyed Mohammad Khatami, statement before the 53rd Session of the General Assembly, 8th plenary meeting, 21 September 1998.

[8] Statement by the representative of Iran, GA/9684, 10 December 1999.

[9] Statement by the representative of Liechtenstein, GA/9684, 10 December 1999.

[10] A/RES/53/22, General Assembly, Fifty-third Session, 16 November 1998.

implement the appropriate cultural, educational, and social programs to promote the concept of dialogue among civilizations. The Secretary General submitted a skeleton report, where he indicated that he intended to respond to the invitation by the Assembly to reflect on the idea of a dialogue among civilizations, and to search for concrete ways to impact the world community. The Secretary General also announced that he had appointed Giandomenico Picco, a former UN official as his Personal Representative for dialogue among civilizations. Mr. Picco, in another skeleton report, made the subject of the preservation of identities and diversity the central theme of the report, and the main objective of the dialogue.

Several speakers took the floor to lend support to the idea of a dialogue among civilizations and referred to one general concept or another, including globalization and its impact, terrorism, tolerance, equality, peace, justice, solidarity, ethnic conflicts, the environment, irrational use of technology, science, education, and mutual respect. They also referred to sovereignty, territorial integrity, understanding, cooperation, pluralism, religious and cultural diversity, democracy, rule of law, constructive co-existence, hegemony, the arms race, cross cultural understanding, and common values.

It was clear from a close examination of the debate of 1998 and 1999 on the question of dialogue among civilizations that this dialogue—the first of its kind—did not reveal any "nouveauté" and that its general character strangely reminded one of the regular General Assembly general debate every fall. The same themes, the same issues as enumerated above were raised and no concrete solutions offered. No one attempted to define the nature of the "dialogue" or the concept of "civilizations", nor were any specific objectives outlined. "Dialogue among civilizations" for what? Why was it necessary to rehash these issues which are debated incessantly every year? Did the speakers who intervened forget about such declarations as the proclamation of 1995 as the Year of Tolerance, of 2000 as the International Year of Peace, or the numerous statements or declarations on the other issues? Can "preserving diversity" inspire anyone, or constitute the leitmotiv of this debate?

Several representatives from Islamic countries that took the floor in the course of 1999 gave the distinct impression of adopting a defensive posture, praising the values of their faith, Islam, in the face of attacks on terrorism which they felt unjustly identified to some extent Islam with violence. The representative of Liechtenstein, while supporting the United Nations as "the perfect forum" for dialogue among civilizations, nevertheless reminded his audience that the Charter provided no clear concept of what a civilization was. He observed that a civilization was a "process", not a "product". He further observed that dialogue among civilizations required the participation of a wide range of actors. "Governments and their policies", he stated, "were expressions of civilizations, but they did not represent them." The main activities associated with the dialogue, he added, should take place outside the intergovernmental framework. The tasks of governments were to provide a forum for such a dialogue, and to "give a voice to those with something to say." [11] As we will see later in this analysis, this statement and a few others constituted in the 1999 debate a rare window in creative thinking about the dialogue among civilizations, a subject which should have excited more than one imagination.

Finland, on behalf of the European Union, proposed to use a wider concept of what constitutes a civilization, "in order to

---

[11] Statement by Liechtenstein, GA/9684, 10 December 1999.

accommodate the varying conditions under which people belonging to different cultures, beliefs, nations—including indigenous people, ethnic, linguistic and religious minorities, and immigrant and refugee communities—met and interacted." [12] The representative of Finland also stated that several instruments were available dealing with tolerance, human rights, cultural cooperation, science and education and formed a strong basis for the dialogue among civilizations. New international instruments were therefore not needed. "What we need," in this representative's view, is "practical action to bring people together by using more modern methods of communication." The representative concluded that, while the European Union supported further development of intergovernmental dialogue in the United Nations system, "it would be disappointed if the Year of Dialogue among Civilizations eventually fell into that category."

In his evaluation of Picco's report, the representative of the Solomon Islands said that "common denominator of values," as formulated by the Representative of the Secretary General, needed further specifying and one wonders whether a consensus on that common denominator could be reached in the near future. The dialogue among civilizations, he observed, raised sensitive questions, and there needs to be a serious dialogue rather than "unanswered monologues." How these matters could be answered could not be left to the Secretariat or a specialized agency to resolve. The dialogue should not be confined to elites at the exclusion of the widest representation of the civil society. [13]

---

[12] Statement by Finland, GA/9684, 10 December 1999.
[13] Statement by the Representative of Solomon Islands, GA/9684, 10 December 1999.

The representative of the Republic of Korea, at the end of the debate in December 1999, noted the existence of universal values. "Those universal values," he said, "were the embodiment of collective wisdom, insights and experiences emanating from different civilizations. They provided rich soil in which the seeds of diversity among civilizations could together be planted and encouraged to flourish." [14]

The representative of the Russian Federation, while agreeing with the conclusion of the report of the Personal Representative of the Secretary General, thought nevertheless that it was "inappropriate to make a distinction between civilizations that perceived diversity as a threat, and those that perceived it as an integral component of growth." Dialogue among civilizations, this representative affirmed, "must be developed as a joint effort of all nations in their struggle against violence, terrorism, poverty, hunger and disease—disasters that denied the very essence and foundations of any civilizations." [15]

ANALYSIS

Reading the first skeleton three-page report of the Secretary General, one quickly realizes that the new theme "dialogue among civilizations" on the General Assembly's agenda simply did not receive the importance that this subject deserves. The report at the outset informs the reader that "the views of other member States [other than Iran] were sought ... and are available for review." No attempt was made to reflect

---

[14] Statement by the Representative of the Republic of Korea, GA/9684.

[15] Statement by the Representative of the Russian Federation, GA/9684, 10 December 1999.

these views or to analyze them. The report warns that "due to the breath of the concept of dialogue among civilizations and the lack of financial resources, any projects to be pursued would have to be extremely focused and supported by funds from outside the United Nations system." [16] The report further indicates that since the concept of dialogue among civilizations has a range of different implications, the number of civilizations is not known, and since there is no definition of a civilization available, "the United Nations may not be the appropriate forum in which to examine them." The authors seem to have forgotten that there was no definition of the concept of "aggression," that the United Nations took many years to agree on such a definition, and that the funds were found for this purpose. The report mentions as a component of the definition of the dialogue among civilizations a cultural dialogue between Islam and the West.   One cannot fail to hypothesize that the funds sought from outside could imply those possibly emanating from the rich Islamic countries of the Arab/Persian Gulf.

And why can't one attempt to define the word "civilization"? Webster's dictionary does it. It defines it as "an ideal state of human culture, characterized by complete absence of barbarism, and non-rational behavior, optimum utilization of physical, cultural, spiritual, and human resources, and perfect adjustment of the individual within the social framework."   The report of the Secretary General does not undertake such a task, and this is puzzling, in view of the fact that the item is officially placed on the agenda of the General Assembly of the United Nations.   Presumably, the report implies   that is   because for governments, the concept of

---

[16] General Assembly, Fifty-fourth session, "United Nations Year of Dialogue among Civilizations", Report of the Secretary General, p.1.

dialogue among civilizations had "different implications." But as is well known, all issues before the United Nations have different implications for member States, and the latter do not seek to transfer them to other forums outside the organization. They engage in long, arduous negotiations to resolve them. The report leaves the reader with the impression that the Secretariat tries to avoid a dialogue on the dialogue among civilizations. This is understandable, since the institution is not intellectually equipped to engage in such a complex, but at the same time, exalting enterprise. It has, however, the capability to gather an eminent group of artists, intellectuals, sociologists, economists, scientists and spiritual leaders to undertake such a task. However, to carry out such an important mission, the group would need to start from premises altogether different from those retained by the Secretariat. While the preservation of diversity is from the cultural point of view a very desirable end, it is by no means the only ultimate goal of a dialogue among civilizations. To reduce the objectives of the dialogue to the preservation of cultural diversity is to reduce the concept to a passive interpretation. Civilization, as one of the representatives noted earlier, is a "process" that is changing, a dynamic phenomenon. Civilizations are born, and they die. New ones emerge over time. And in our times, the times of globalization, regional integration, and convergence, a new civilization with new values, such as global solidarity, seems to be emerging on the horizon. It is the civilization that connects among countries and peoples and their environment, one that would place the human person at the center of its activities, in terms of his/her intellectual, social and cultural development. To examine the nature of this new civilization, capture its essence, attempt to clarify the values that accompany it, and delineate its role in the resolution of humankind's problems in the new millennium constitute an edifying task, not a bureaucratic exercise.

FRAMEWORK FOR DIALOGUE AMONG CIVILIZATIONS

What is a civilization? It can be defined in a variety of ways. A civilization can be viewed as the historical creation of an advanced community or society in the institutional, technological, educational, cultural, and artistic fields, whose contribution transcends its borders and is enduring. Therefore, we can speak of the Chinese, French, or Mayan civilization. A civilization implies historical roots and a broad movement of progress in all human endeavors. Civilization connotes an organized structure, a language, a culture, values, customs, and traditions, and, above all, the gift of creation.

Can civilizations dialogue with each other? Yes, in a relative sense. Two pieces of music can speak or react to each other. At one of the recent events in the Hall of the General Assembly of the United Nations, Secretary General Kofi Annan sought to include in a classical music orchestra the talents of a Jazz artist, who accompanied the orchestra. Those in the audience that believed in the possibility of marrying classical music with music of another genre—Jazz in this case—applauded this common language. Those who did not approve, quietly decried the event. An art exhibit with tableaus from both the East and the West can create a powerful impression. In the political sense, however, in the sense that dialogue among nations has been introduced as an item at the United Nations, only representatives from nations are at present engaged in the dialogue. Government representatives, however, cannot claim to embody their civilization, which is much broader than the political arena. Not even Cabinet Ministers of Culture can claim that privilege. Civilizations can only be represented by their creators—that is, historians, thinkers, philosophers, writers, economists, scientists, men and women of literature, musicians, poets, and of course, managers and leaders, both political and spiritual.

This leads us to another important characteristic of civilizations: their multi-dimensionality. To conduct a dialogue among civilizations, it would therefore be essential to ensure a wide participation of representatives from the various fields enumerated above. In other words, civil society must join the political representatives to ensure a comprehensive and genuine dialogue. A new form of political representation should therefore be considered by the United Nations.

At the Secretariat level, thought should be given to broadening the leadership of the dialogue among civilizations to include the major spiritual sensitivities. The East and the West, spiritual leaders, intellectuals, artists and other fields should join their efforts in a small but broadly representative Civilization Forum whose task would be to examine the various ways in which the major civilizations can contribute concretely to the main issues facing humanity today: peace, disarmament, the environment, poverty and disease.

Towards that objective, the Civilization Forum (CF) can set up a Civilization Council (CC) to examine closely new forms of international cooperation necessitated by the advent of the globalization, integration, and convergence process now underway. The CC would in particular address itself to the delineation of the common values of civilizations which would serve as means for the strengthening of global solidarity. The CC would act as a mobile vehicle, which would travel to various capitals of the world to hold hearings, gather ideas and documents, and draw up reports for the CF. The latter would advise the Secretary General on the basis of those reports, who would then draft his own report to the General Assembly.

This broad representation can contribute to strengthening the bonds of diverse civilizations, to linking various professions and fields, and enhancing the sense of solidarity among the large communities in the world. Spiritual and moral leaders can be called upon to use their moral influence and act as the Ambassadors for the Dialogue among Civilizations to heighten the sense of responsibility and commitment in the resolution of humankind's major issues, as listed above.

An Expert Group on Civilizations (EGC) can be established within UNESCO to study the contribution made by various civilizations in the world, and, simultaneously, examine the nature and characteristics of the emerging new civilization. For example, the EGC would analyze the impact of the Egyptian or Greek civilization, but, also, closely scrutinize the features of the slowly emerging integrated European civilization consequent to the establishment of the European Union.

A dialogue among civilizations can lead to the preservation of diversity and to mutual understanding of old, present, and emerging civilizations, but it can also seek to speak a common language. At the present stage of human development, such a common language cannot be found in the political, economic, technological or even cultural field. Such a common language, however, already exists in the arts, especially music. Music speaks the language of every community and civilization and should be used as a vehicle to cement the bonds of our common humanity.

A major task of the CF would consist in strengthening the ties between cultures and civilizations through the annual holding of a Civilization Music Concert (CMC) at the United Nations Headquarters, which would bring together the best artists from the major civilizations in the world. Such an event would be broadcast throughout the world via an arrangement worked out with a major television network such as CNN or directly through a newly established Civilization T.V. established by the United Nations. It would also help open the doors of the United Nations to Civil Society and enhance its image among the world community.

It would be most useful for the Dialogue among civilizations if it were to open a Civilization Website to receive communications from Civil Society.

If member States consider the Iranian President's proposal on the dialogue among civilizations to be an important subject, they should arrange for the funds necessary for its implementation to be provided both from within the existing resources of the United Nations and outside foundations and personalities. They should welcome the contributions to be made in the context of this item by actors outside the United Nations and their role in the consolidation of peace, in disarmament, and in tackling the issues of the environment, poverty, and disease. The General Assembly could adopt a declaration calling on all civilizations to mobilize their communities in these pursuits and to signify to the Secretary General of the United Nations the nature of their concrete commitments.

To make its utmost contribution to the practical resolution of one of the universal scourges of human degradation, the dialogue among civilizations could focus its efforts on the crucial issue of poverty. To aim for its elimination from all areas of the world where it exists in the next twenty-five years would constitute one of its noblest missions. [17] Poverty

---

[17] One in three Africans is hungry everyday. A quarter of Africa' children

degrades the human being, and deprives the human person of his/her right to a decent life. In the present stage of humankind's development, poverty will increasingly become morally unacceptable. All civilizations have the sensitivities, are endowed with the necessary compassion, and are capable of engaging in commitments to make the elimination of poverty from the face of the globe the greatest spiritual battle of the 21st century. Civilizations possess the intrinsic ingredients to touch people's heart and soul, and to enable them to turn their indifference into commitments. Moral and spiritual leaders have the capacity and the vision to inspire large segments of people to undertake tasks that are both beyond their self-centeredness and are self fulfilling.

CONCLUSION

The "Dialogue among Civilizations" introduced at the United Nations by President Khatami offers the world community a unique opportunity to join hands in inaugurating the advent of new forms of global cooperation. The dialogue can be used as an instrument for the preservation of the diversity and richness of past and present cultures and civilizations. Beyond that, the dialogue could serve as a basis for delineating and understanding the dimensions of the slowly emerging new civilization of the new age. It can act as a

---

will die before their fifth birthday of disease and malnutrition. Africa is home to nearly a quarter of the 790 million undernourished people in the world. This means that most sub-Saharan African countries cannot adequately feed between 30 and 70 per cent of their populations. Africa is the only continent where food insecurity is expected to increase. Four out of ten Africans live in absolute poverty and recent evidence suggests that poverty is on the rise. *World Food Aid in Africa*, Rome, 18 January 2000.

vehicle for deeper understanding among the various cultures in the world. The dialogue among civilizations is capable of transforming itself from a passive forum to an active instrument by participating effectively in the resolution of some of humankind's burning issues.

The discourse among cultures and nations can lead to new forms of representation in the global forums and of new forms of global cooperation to liberate human beings from the scourge of poverty so that they can regain their dignity and truly enjoy the blessings of liberty. To achieve these objectives, the dialogue needs to broaden its leadership, develop a framework, focus its work, and secure the necessary resources.

The Secretary General of the United Nations, Mr. Kofi Annan, in a message to the meeting of the Foreign Ministers of the Organization of the Islamic Conference (OIC) held on 28 June 1999 in Ouagadougou, Burkina Faso, characterized the dialogue as follows:

> The dialogue among civilizations must be peaceful. It must occur not just between societies but within them. It must be a dialogue of mutual respect, based on a framework of shared values—values such as those found in the United Nations Charter, like equality, justice and dignity—within which different traditions can co-exist. Such a dialogue can serve as an inspiration to all humanity. It can help us learn from each other. It can help us rise above the intolerance and conflicts that have blighted our history and undermined human progress.[18]

The dialogue among civilizations must not be identified

---

[18] Text of the message of Secretary General Kofi Annan to the Twenty-sixth Session of Foreign Ministers of the Organization of the Islamic Conference, SG/SM/7050, 28 June 1999.

with a political dialogue, which requires a compromise. Because it concerns the precious treasures of nations—their civilizations—it operates, or should operate, at a higher level, on the basis of sublimity and nobleness. Above all, the dialogue among civilizations should seek to identify and give life to those higher values that define our common humanity and that led Latin poet Terence to proclaim, "I am a man, and nothing that touches the human condition would leave me indifferent." Its death would be brought by sterility; its success, by creativity. Its ultimate objective should be the strengthening of human solidarity and the humanization of global relations.

THE ROLE OF RELIGION IN THE DIALOGUE AMONG CIVILIZATIONS

William Vendley, Ph.D.

Dr. William F. Vendley is the Secretary-General of the World Conference on Religion and Peace/International (WCRP). The organization is the largest worldwide coalition of representatives of religious communities. In WCRP, religious representatives - respectful of their differences in belief - work together to take common actions to address critical problems in areas such as conflict resolution, human rights and development. Dr. Vendley is a member of the Governing Board and serves as the Executive Director of the Secretariat. In the latter capacity, he oversees all international projects, coordinates staff in WCRP offices around the world, and assists members in 35 national chapters and in over 100 countries.

INTRODUCTION

A concrete image taken from a single religion and a particular civilization can provide an insight, which if applied analogically, may be useful to think about the more general role of religion in the dialogue among civilizations.

Consider if you will a "double" image involving the late Rev. Dr. Martin Luther King. First, imagine Rev. King, a Christian minister, preaching in a small church in the south of the United States about racism. As a believer speaking with fellow believers, Rev. King engages the resources of their shared religious tradition. He preaches as a Christian among Christians, and with this group of believers he speaks in the language of their religion, creatively engaging, re-working, and re-expressing its sources and traditions. As he speaks, their hearts burn with a passion for justice based on their religious convictions.

Next, follow Dr. King as he leaves the small church and steps out on his nation's mall in Washington D.C. Spread out before him are more than a half a million persons. Each gathered there is concerned about civil rights. Some are Christians, others are Jews, Muslims, Hindus, Buddhists, or members of other religions, and still others profess no religion at all. Dr. King cannot simply repeat the sermon he gave in the church. He cannot engage this plural group with his Christian sectarian religious language, for many in the group do not share his religious tradition. Dr. King has to speak some kind of "public" language. He has to creatively re-express the moral concerns expressed in his church sermon in public language. Standing in the public square, Dr. King makes his case against racism in public terms, speaking of civil rights, and he supports his case with public warrants. His speech is compelling. The group locks arms in solidarity as an expression of common cause.

When both aspects of the double image are entertained simultaneously, we find a single religious person prosecuting his religiously rooted moral concern in two different languages: one sectarian and the other public. Although the image involves only one religion and one civilization, an understanding of the interaction of these two languages can, I suggest, offer a clue on how we might better understand the role of religion in the dialogue among civilizations.

BIAS

It is best to state my bias up front. I do not expect a single "universal" civilization to eclipse all diverse civilizations.[1] While I believe a kind of universal civilization has begun to emerge and will continue to develop, I also believe diversity will remain part of our experience. The deeper question lies in the character of the relationship of different civilizations to the emerging universal one.   Will the emerging universal civilization consist of only a "thin" universality, largely if not solely based on technological reason and economic globalization?   Or, could there emerge an ever "thicker" universal civilization based upon each particular civilization's contributions to the common good? My bias is for the latter. However, for such a prospect to flourish each civilization would be challenged to effectively mediate its cultural genius

---

[1] Nor do I expect the plurality of religions to be superceded by a single religion.

to an emerging universal civilization. Like Dr. King as he stood before the diverse group on his nation's mall, particular civilizations would have to learn how to mediate their specific legacies in public terms meaningful and accessible to those outside of the swath of their own civilization.

In such a vision, particular civilizations and an emerging universal one would remain in constructive and mutually transformative tension. Peoples would increasing abide both by their particular civilizations and by an ever-thicker universal one.[2] Peoples would increasingly learn to become bi-lingual, capable of using the dynamic language of their original civilization within the swath of that civilization and, as well, capable of using and contributing to the development of an increasingly rich public language related to the emergence of an ever-thicker universal civilization. Such a prospect would require collective creativity, but has not this creativity already been amply manifested in the building up of civilizations across time? If so, why should not this creativity today be expressed in the ongoing development of a form of "dual civilizational citizenship" with an accompanying ongoing development of a related bi-lingual capacity?

How, then, can religion give us an insight into the possibility of an ever "thicker" universal civilization emerging out of, co-abiding with, and even stimulating the further unfolding of existing civilizations? To start, we must first examine a couple of basic notions.

---

[2] Increasingly, some persons are able to abide in two or more of the historic civilizations as well as the emerging universal one. For simplicity of illustration, we restrict ourselves to two civilizations.

CULTURE, CIVILIZATION, AND RELIGION

A normative notion of culture has been largely displaced by an empirical notion. If the older normative notion of culture distinguished between those who "had culture" and those deemed to be "uncultured," an empirical notion of culture drops any sense of normativity.[3] The empirical notion understands culture as a shared set of meanings and values that define a common way of life.[4] Concretely, these shared meanings and values are mediated across time to successive generations by language, habits, mores, customs, traditions, and institutions. In the empirical definition, there are as many cultures as there are sets of shared meanings and values.

Civilization is also a cultural reality, and it can be thought of as culture "writ large." Civilization is notable for its scope and swath.[5] While all civilizations are an expression of culture, not all cultures generate civilizations. Civilization, it can be argued, is the broadest cultural entity. According to the British historian Arnold Toynbee, civilizations comprehend without being comprehended; they are a totality.[6] According to this view, Chinese, Hindus, and European Christians partake of distinct civilizations and do not belong to any broader cultural

---

[3] For all of its value in overcoming cultural hegemony, an empirical notion of culture has it limits insofar as it systematically avoids "truth claims." Some form of shared normative notion of truth would seem to be essential for any culture or civilization, including an emerging universal civilization.

[4] Bernard Lonergan, *Method in Theology*, New York: Herder and Herder, 1972.

[5] Samual P. Huntington, *The Clash of Civilizations and the Remaking of World Order*, New York: Simon and Schuster, 1996, p. 42.

[6] Quoted in Huntington, p. 42.

entity.[7] Moreover, these and other civilizations are also notable for their duration across time. They have long historical continuity.[8]

Religion and civilization are related *de facto*. It has been persuasively argued that religion is the most defining characteristic of civilization.[9] It is a matter of fact that to date, all of the great civilizations are intimately related to religion. So intimate is the relationship that it has been observed that "the great religions are the foundations on which the great civilizations rest."[10]

A brief examination of the foundational character of religion can shed some light on its intimate association to civilizations.

First, virtually all religions engage in their own unique ways in the prosecution of two exceptionally radical and encompassing questions: those dealing with pathology and soteriology.[11] Questions of pathology deal with an examination and explanation of what is wrong with the present state of affairs. They attempt to make an explanatory account of the manifest disorder of our experience of reality. They try to make sense of concrete experiences of human tragedy, frailty, vulnerability, the oppressive experience of cruelty and wickedness, and their distorting effects upon social order.

---

[7] In the view of this author, Toynbee's position needs to be nuanced if in fact there is a genuine emergence of a universal civilization that will co-exist with previously existing civilizations.

[8] Ibid, p. 43.

[9] Ibid. p. 47.

[10] Christopher Dawson, *Dynamics of World History*, p. 128, as quoted in Huntington, p. 47.

[11] Religions also invariably inquire after the origin and destiny of human reality.

Paralleling the examination of pathology, matching its depth and responding to it, religions invariably engage in questions of soteriology (salvation). These questions inquire after the means by which the experience of pathology can be overcome. They ponder how the deepest source(s) of reality can assist in the re-orientation of personal and communal praxis so as to overcome the deepest levels of disorder disclosed in a given religion's analysis of pathology.

The radicality of these questions, and the fact that they are prosecuted across time, gives these religious questions the power to provide a foundation for the shared meanings and values that constitute civilizations. Moreover, these two questions are typically combined to give religions their technically "utopic" quality. Religions proffer normative, if typically anticipatory or heuristic, visions of how peoples are called to live. They provide an inclusive vision of the meaning of human community and its position and role in the cosmos. Thus, it is perhaps not surprising that these religious visions, including the way they call people to live and orient themselves in reality, are foundational to the birth and development of civilizations.

THE NARRATIVE STRUCTURE OF RELIGION

"We tell ourselves stories in order to live," writes Joan Didion.[12] Human life is somehow given its most elemental identity by story or narrative. "For we dream in narrative, daydream in narrative, remember, anticipate, hope, despair, believe, doubt, plan, revise, criticize, construct, gossip, learn,

---

[12]Joan Didion, *The White Album* (New York: Simon & Schuster, 1979), p. 11.

hate and love by narrative," says Barbara Hady.[13] It is a story or narrative structure which provides overarching coherence to the diversity of experience and which grounds the set of meanings and values by which people can coherently live. All things human refer to a narrative story of some kind. Both individuals and -- one must especially stress -- the cultures and civilizations that form them are shaped in a most foundational and elemental way by narrative.

What is true of civilizations and other cultures is also the case with religions. Religions, too, are organized around central stories and narratives. These narratives can be mediated or transmitted in a variety of ways. They can be passed on orally, by means of sacred texts, through learned commentaries or elaborate and penetrating systems of thought based upon sacred texts, through rituals or forms of prayer and meditation, and by means of a variety of other carriers of meaning such as music, song and dance. For example, for Dr. King, a Christian, the central narratives are the Jewish and Christian Biblical texts. There are many different stories in the Bible, but they combine into an overarching narrative of God's redemption of history. But in Christianity this overarching narrative is "filled out" by the myriad expressions of its meaning which, collectively and across time, have attempted to offer an account of the meaning of God's relationship with history consistent with the vision of the Scriptures. In their

---

[13] Barbara Hady, quoted in Wicker, *The Story-shaped World: Fiction and Metaphysics: Some Variations on a Theme* (Notre Dame, Ind.: University of Notre Dame Press, 1975), p. 4. The writer first encountered this quote in Charles V. Gerkin, *Widening the Horizons: Pastoral Responses to a Fragmented Society* (Philadelphia: The Westminster Press, 1986), p. 29. Gerkin's book explores the importance of narrative for Pastoral Theology. I wish to acknowledge the positive impact of Gerkin's work on my attempt to reflect on the impact of narrative on multireligious cooperation.

own distinctive ways, Hinduism, Buddhism, Judaism, Islam, and the other religions have their own sets of stories, which combine for each of them into an overarching narrative that provides the deepest base and fertile foundation of each particular religion's interpretations of reality. Importantly, religious narratives can be recognized as founding a particular religious tradition's understanding of ethical responsibility and providing its followers with norms and principles for a requisite moral stance in life.

The deep stories which combine into an organizing or overarching narrative of a given religion, however they are understood by a particular religious tradition, I wish to designate as that religion's *primary language.* Primary language, in my use of the term, is the language that founds and defines a religious community. Thus each religious community has its own primary language or interpretations of primary language. This language provides the deep story that gives a religious community its specific identity. Primary religious language constitutes the core of the living memory of a religious community, it offers the grammar of identity, it provides for the possibility of shared experience and a shared interpretation of experience, it installs a community of believers in a shared moral space, and it provides a fertile foundation for the community's passage through time, orienting it both to the past, present and future.[14]

---

[14] Paul Ricoeur notes that our experience of time has a narrative structure. We experience time as a story with a past, a present and a future. See Paul Ricoeur, *Time and Narrative* vol. 1 (Chicago: University of Chicago Press, 1984), p. 52.

CREATIVE RELIGIOUS FIDELITY

The development of highly elaborated religious traditions across time gives ample evidence to religious creativity. This creativity, in turn, can be recognized to be intimately related to civilizational creativity. A general notion of how religious communities have creatively responded to challenges across time can provide insight regarding the demands for religious creativity today, especially in relationship to the emergence of an ever-thicker universal civilization.

Confronted with new challenges, religious communities[15] often respond by engaging in two highly creative sets of activities.[16] On the one hand, they are driven back into the roots of their own histories, back to their central religious stories. The new experience, if it is to be grasped by a given religious community, needs to be interpreted in relationship to the primary language of that community. Perhaps not all stories in the primary language appear immediately helpful in the sense that they can be readily connected with the new problem at hand. The community is driven back in search of a "usable past." What story, what chapter of a story, what teachings or practices embodied in at least some episode of the overarching narrative of a particular religious tradition can help orient contemporary believers before the new situation they

---

[15] Our description is general. In fact, there are typically many voices in any one religious community, and creative advances are often accompanied by considerable tension among diverse strands in a community.

[16] These two types of activities are not necessarily distinguished by all religious communities in accord with our analysis. However, attention to the actual performances of religious communities indicates that they engage in two such activities, however interpreted, to at least a limited degree, if they are functioning in relationship to contemporary problems in any fashion at all.

face? This task of "turning back" to listen to or "hear" the narratives of a religious tradition from the perspective of a new problem or situation is itself a highly creative activity. The religious community has to work out a connection, to discover a correlation, between pertinent elements within its storehouse of religious narrative and a new situation.[17]

On the other hand, each religious community must also move forward in relationship to the new challenge. It has to try to "say anew" what it has "heard" of the tradition in relationship to the new crisis being faced. To really say anew what it means to be a faithful believer in relationship to a new challenge requires a dynamically creative set of acts that orient believers affectively, cognitively, morally, and spiritually before the new crisis. By saying anew we mean not just words but the total religious response in words and multiple other actions, including the re-orientation of institutional assets, which address the many dimensions of the problem or challenge being faced.

How, then, does a religious community say anew what it means to be faithful religiously when confronting a new major challenge? Today, there are two distinct spheres of answering, corresponding to two types of language, primary (sectarian) and secondary (public) language. Each sphere is an arena for creative religious action. The latter, I would argue, is essential if religions are going to successfully mediate their rich legacies

---

[17] The fact that religious communities are challenged to search for a usable past, something within their collective store of narrative that connects with a current challenge, offers a clue as to how religions can subtly change their major foci over time. What previously may have been a comparatively minor story in a tradition can, due to its relevance to a major historical challenge, begin to assume an ever-greater relative importance within a given religious tradition.

to an emerging universal civilization.

Creativity in Primary Language

Members of religious communities speak among themselves. Religious primary language is employed again and again across time to continuously say anew what it means to be a religious believer within one's own circle of believers. Across time and in every new place, believers are challenged to correlate their primary language with contemporary realities so that new insights can be achieved into what it means to be a responsible believer in relationship to the circumstances and challenges at hand. This extended conversation bears fruit by clarifying believers' moral sensibilities in relationship to new circumstances and guiding them into related responsible forms of action precisely as believers working among themselves.

On the one hand, the great strength of saying anew one religious identity in one's primary language is the depth, elemental strength, and extraordinary fecundity of primary language, evidenced in its ability to continually secure the religious identities of believers and to re-orient them morally in the constantly changing vicissitudes of history.

On the other hand, speaking is primary speech, for all its force and richness, limits one, for the most part, to the circle of believers who share the same language. Primary language is a not a language for engagement of others in either multireligious cooperation or in the public arena.

Creativity in Secondary Pubic Language

Today religious communities do not restrict the expressions of their ultimate concern to their own members. Under the pressures of religious and secular forms of pluralism and through the engagement of urgent issues, which involve more than a single community, representatives of religious communities are now learning to speak a secondary public language of moral care beyond their particular circle of believers. Many religious communities now feel compelled by their own sense of the truth and universal relevance of their central stories to "speak their concerns" in the public arena by translating, or better transposing, the ethical sensibilities, which are rooted, in their respective primary languages into a secondary public language.[18]

Public language, no less than a given primary language, is dynamic; it develops, changes, and grows over time. Thus, religions cannot simply adopt so-called "secular" language as the finished form of public language. On the one hand, much of secular language is freighted with an "antireligious" bias. The word secular is often interpreted to intend a social sphere bereft of religious dimensions of meaning. On the other hand, and on a more positive note, what we currently call secular language needs to be developed into a richer and fuller public language, increasingly capable of expressing matters of ultimate concern in public terms. At its deepest level, the creative transposition of religious primary language into forms

---

[18] Indeed, there has been a long tradition in some societies and religious communities of notions of natural law, that attempt to give expression to an intelligible moral sphere available to human intelligence without the direct assistance of religion. This intelligible moral sphere has been recognized as a basis for the organization of a non-sectarian understanding of political order. Today, however, there is no widely shared consensus about natural law or related forms of juris prudence. In its stead, the notion of human rights -- as set forth in international declarations and covenants -- provides a slender but essential area of public social moral consensus expressed in public language. Increasingly the world's religions are learning to root the notions of human rights in their own rich primary languages.

of public language can be a profoundly creative stimulus toward the creation of an ever richer, historically rooted, and more morally nuanced public language.

Speaking in public language calls religious communities to express their moral concerns in a new way, by calling them to provide public warrants for their moral positions. In the arena of public life, each religious community can make its claims regarding matters of ultimate concern by appealing to their rationality and cogency for public life. Public language allows religious persons to make public commitments to the common good and support those public commitments with public warrants, even though the original (and sustaining) motivations for their commitments and respective rationales remain anchored in their respective religious resources.

There is an enormous advantage for religious communities in being able to speak a secondary public language. First, when different religious communities express their ultimate senses of caring through the employment of secondary public language, these different religious communities can often discern important areas of moral convergence. Indeed, a shared secondary language artfully employed by different religious communities can provide to them a medium to clarify agreements on matters of moral concern and a basis for cooperative action. Of equal importance, a shared secondary language also allows different religious communities to clarify where they disagree on important moral issues. With a shared secondary language, religious communities are given the freedom to agree on some issues and disagree on others, without violating the religiously normative character of their respective primary languages.[19] Secondary language provides

---

[19] More generally, the religious employment of secondary language

a medium that avoids the dangers of either conflating or failing to respect the "differences" of different primary religious languages.

Secondary public language provides a medium, which in its own way functions as a formal condition, for multireligious cooperation. Indeed, it can be the medium for religious communities to work on the public good in a fully public fashion, in partnership with all men and women of good will who share similar value orientations.

The creativity involved in learning to speak a public language is uniquely useful to assisting religious communities to work collaboratively for the common good. Similar creativity must be exercised in re-imagining the panoply of religious institutions if they are to be marshaled in public attempts to build up the common good. For, just as each religious community is challenged to become "bi-lingual," thereby retaining both its identity in the language that unites its believers *and* resaying its care in public terms, so, too, there is the challenge to reimagine religious institutions in terms of dual use: both continuing to serve profoundly the specific needs of their communities *and* as exceptional assets for the common good.

---

provides the key to understanding how communal beliefs, be they religious or non-religious, can be related to public life in "secular" societies. The use of secondary public language allows religious or other ideological communities to express their concerns in the public square side by side with other men and women of good will, regardless of their particular religious or ideological convictions.

ROLE OF RELIGION IN THE POLITICAL ORDER

How, then, can religions contribute to the possibility of the development of an ever-thicker universal civilization emerging out of, co-abiding with, and even stimulating the further unfolding of existing civilizations? The answer, in short, is to recognize that religions are in fact learning how to both retain their identities (and therefore their relationships with the civilization to which they are intimately related) *and* to express their commitments in wider, often global, public arenas (and therefore forging new relationships with and contributing to an emerging universal civilization). To the extent religions continue to express their concerns in both ways, they will continue to contribute to the mutually creative dialogue among civilizations toward an ever-thicker universal civilization. To do both, religions need to continue to develop their capacities for creative bi-lingual expression. For, only the employment of a primary language can provide historical continuity to a religious-civilizational legacy, while only the employment of a secondary public language can mediate the riches of such a legacy to those who do not espouse it as their own.

One example seems especially relevant, the question of political order, specifically the question of a global political order by which different states related to different civilizations can flourish together. For, if religion provides a foundation for civilization, the latter, in turn, develops shared meanings and values that are given expression in political institutions that serve particular notions of political order. The question arises, then, regarding the development of a notion of political order that can be constructively informed by and serve diverse religious-civilizational heritages.

The question should not lead to a confusion of religion or civilization with government, let alone an emerging universal civilization with a universal government. Civilizations are cultural not political entities. "They do not, as such, maintain order, establish justice, collect taxes, fight wars, negotiate treaties, or do any of the other things that governments do."[20] Nevertheless, religions and civilizations impact notions of political order, which in turn are served by political institutions that express the meanings and values of a given culture and civilization. Therefore, it is worthwhile to examine very briefly the relationship of religion to political order.

Critical proponents of all particular religions and civilizations now know that they cannot make a final claim to determine political order for everyone. Historically, religions have fought each other, often over the question of political order. This contributed significantly to the Enlightenment's separation of Religion from State, an arrangement that is increasingly adopted around the world, especially in countries with religiously plural populations. In this arrangement, typically no religion is given entitlement by the State, and the moral basis for political order is no longer founded formally upon a religion, but upon an Enlightenment version of a commitment to some form of public rationality. In short, religion is formally removed from the public arena. Religious commitments and the intellectual "warrants" for belief are to be kept out of public life and decision-making. One may believe in one's religion if one wants, but that is increasingly an individual and private affair.

Although the Enlightenment's reasons for the banishment of religions from the public arena were many, believers themselves are often the first to acknowledge that religion was very often abused when it was fused with the state. Religious

---

[20] Huntington, p. 44.

intolerance and the rejection of pluralism was only one manifestation of the disorder to which a fused religion-state relation was prone.

Notwithstanding its merits, think with me in broad strokes of the limits of the Enlightenment arrangement: Religion remains formally banished from the public arena.   Ever more limited forms of rationality, particularly technical rationality and its economic correlates, reign as the basis of political and economic order.   The vast and subtle realms of human memory contained especially in the world's religions remain formally relegated to the sidelines.   A peculiar form of amnesia rules public life, insofar as religions, understood as the great receptacles of communal memory, are deemed irrelevant to public life and its challenges.   The public tries to face the future by making a social compact to formally forget the past, insofar as it resides in religious carriers of meaning that have been used and in fact have defined most of human history.

On the other hand, think with me of the religions finding a safe way to re-enter the public arena together.   Surely one religion cannot dominate the others as was the temptation in the past.   Surely the public arena will still require public forms of rationality, but need they necessarily be reductive?   Must public language necessarily be closed to the realms of meaning to which religious languages refer?   Could not public language be creatively engaged and transformed by the religions?   Could not this transformation of public language both respect its non-sectarian character, yet still assist public language to more nearly approximate the moral ranges that religious languages know to be essential to humanity?   If the religions can find appropriate ways to re-enter the public arena, that arena itself becomes the locus of historical continuity and encounter.   All that was good in previous human experience becomes an analogue to inform the creativity of spirit we need in our own day. In this scenario, memory, deep memory of what it means to be a human being in community, instead of public amnesia, becomes a resource for our collective creativity. If religions can find a safe way to re-enter the public arena, it would suggest that the Enlightenment solution of effectively keeping religion out of the public square might be more of a "creative pause" than an historical end point.

The religious engagement of secondary public language is the way for religions to re-enter the public arena to address the fundamental challenges that confront the human family. Today, this public arena is increasingly global. Today, what needs to be forged is an ever-thicker universal set of meaning and values that can inform common ways of life, in short, a universal civilization.   Religions, the great repositories of memory, the foundations of civilizations, are now beginning to mediate their riches into the public arena in public terms. They are learning to both retain their primary languages and to speak a secondary public language. To the extent that they continue to do so, they will continue to both strengthen existing civilizational legacies and help to transpose those deep legacies into a common heritage in the service of the common good.

SPIRITUAL AND PSYCHOLOGICAL DIMENSIONS OF A NEW CIVILIZATION

Nancy B. Roof, Ph.D.

Dr. Nancy B. Roof is the author of several articles on values, ethics, and spirituality in global issues, and has lectured widely to international professional organizations, receiving awards for her contributions. She is the author of *The Impact of War on Service Providers.* She was founding Co-Chair of the Values Caucus at the United Nations. Her testimony to the U.S. commission on Improving the Effectiveness of the UN was included in the final report sent to the U.S, President and Congress. She represents The Center for Psychology and Social Change (an affiliate of Harvard Medical School) in consultative status with the United Nations.

"The future enters into us, in order to transform itself in us, long before it happens"

Rainer Maria Rilke

INTRODUCTION

The following article offers a psychological and spiritual perspective on a new civilization. The ultimate value of the article depends on whether or not it serves as a springboard to the reader's own ideas and actions. It consists of four parts.

The Need: Clarity, Vision and Direction in a Changing World discusses the confusion and insecurity that is characteristic of living in rapidly changing times. It suggests that understanding and accepting that the historical context in which we live is a transitional one between an old and a new era, can lead to psychological security. Security comes not from holding on to the old, or prematurely moving into the new, but in accepting the opportunities afforded by the transitional state of the times to consciously direct the forces of change towards higher values. The apparent breakdown of some of our institutions and the lowering of borders offers us an opportunity to build a new global civilization. The choices we make today are crucial; they can lead to the fulfillment of our most exalted hopes or to the mutual destruction of our planet. We live in a critical moment in time.

Old Paradigm Meets New Paradigm: Sweeping Evolutionary Advances describes the sweeping evolutionary advances that have precipitated radical changes in our worldview. The external forces of change include the new discoveries in physics concerning the nature of matter, modern technologies, the growth of transnational corporations, and other global trends. Paralleling these trends is an increased urgency for reexamining values, ethics, and spirituality. Finally, this part of the article offers some ideas about the interconnection between the changing nature of consciousness that parallel changes in the material world. It will be based on the work of the American Philosopher, Ken Wilber, and will look at the concept of the parallel evolution between inner and outer forces. The difference between the old paradigm based on the idea of separateness of all entities is contrasted with the new paradigm of synthetic wholeness, consisting of separate, but related parts of a larger whole. The significance of this change is discussed in the context of its impact on the individual and the collective.

Learning to Live Together: Dialogue Among Civilizations and Universal Values in International Affairs introduces some ideas on how we can direct the forces of change. In answer to Samuel Huntington's *The Clash of Civilizations and the Remaking of the World Order,* [1] the United Nations has designated the year 2001 as the Year of Dialogue among Civilizations. This innovative United Nations effort can begin the process of harmonizing diverse cultures and civilizations. This section discusses some considerations that psychology can offer to that dialogue. It identifies the differences between levels of consciousness and values that create clashes and misunderstandings between individuals and the collective. It suggests that in addition to dialogues between cultures, differences in values within cultures based on differing levels of understanding is worth considering. Finally it deals with commonalities at the international level, by suggesting the need to place universal and spiritual values at the center of international affairs.

---

[1] Huntington, Samuel, *The Clash of Civilizations and the Remaking of the World Order.* Simon & Schuster, 1997.

Individual and Collective Challenges for a Global Society: Towards a New Civilization discusses individual and collective approaches to change. It suggests further important changes in inner consciousness, relating to others, and relating to the whole, which affect individual, group, and international relations. It includes emerging values such as empowerment, self-determination, transparency, solidarity, planetary citizenship, inner peace, and social responsibility. It suggests some new ideas, attitudes, and approaches that can be helpful in directing the forces of change for the common good.

The Conclusion integrates the ideas in the paper and suggests some educational and organizational steps needed for implementation.

CLARITY, VISION, AND DIRECTION IN A CHANGING WORLD

There is a sense of excitement as well as angst as we encounter the unprecedented speed of the rapid and profound changes in our lives. These changes are a source of riches for some, but for most they are a source of suffering and pain. We are heading towards a global civilization and are just beginning to learn how to humanize this potential development. We have paid allegiance to our families, communities, and states in the past. Now life asks us to make an even more inclusive expansion and identify ourselves as world citizens in a global society, with all the responsibilities that implies. Understanding our place in history is essential for peace of mind. We are asked not only to understand, but also to fully *accept* the times in which we live. Our psychological security depends on our capacity to identify the trends of the times, evaluate them, and to find ways to influence the direction of these trends for the common good.

However, during these critical times, many experience confusion, insecurity, and dissatisfaction on individual, community, national, global and spiritual levels.   On the individual level, there is confusion as to what to believe in and therefore how to make choices and to take action. The large number of individuals, groups, and states whose ultimate value seems to be self-interest and self-fulfillment bewilders us.   In international relations, in particular, self-interest seems to be the acceptable norm.   In our communities and states we notice an alarming gap between the rich and poor, cynicism of the media, increasing violence, drugs, crime and a host of problems which threaten to overwhelm our security.   We recognize that global problems affect all of humanity, our planetary home, and even our survival.   At the spiritual level many individuals live their daily lives with a lack of meaning, purpose, and inspiration, bereft of motivation and hope.

Clarity of thought, vision of a possible positive direction, and realistic acceptance of the present have tremendous power to heal our inner and outer turmoil. The uneven distribution of the riches and benefits of globalization, plus the increasing capacity to destroy our planet and ourselves, are threats we must address.   The urgency of the times requires making a commitment to change the direction of forces towards the good, the true, and the beautiful for all living creatures. We do not need to be powerless victims of impersonal forces, but can choose to take responsibility and become creators of our own destiny.

A most hopeful trend is the increasing interconnection and unity in the world. We now realize that unresolved problems and injustices will impact us all. International civil society is quickly building, as it has become clear that global problems can only be solved through global means. Humanitarian movements are bringing people together from all over the planet. There are movements to share our material and spiritual resources. A new consciousness is building that truly understands that your success is my success, your pain is my pain, and your joys are my joys.

One of the immediate tasks is to view change in a positive manner. Letting go of the fear of change seems to be a universally difficult undertaking, and one that must be consciously practiced. Inner discipline and changing attitudes are needed if we are to master the debilitating effects of fear. Yet the benefits will lessen confusion and give the space to move from a passive and victim consciousness of unbridled forces to one of strength and responsibility. We can view our changing times as an opportunity to participate in building a better world.

OLD PARADIGM MEETS NEW PARADIGM

"There is nothing more powerful than an idea whose time has come"

Victor Hugo

Sweeping evolutionary changes have occurred in only a few decades. The changes are profound and transformative in their impact, affecting both our external and internal lives. We are moving from an old paradigm to a new one. The term "paradigm" was coined in the groundbreaking work of Thomas Kuhn, a philosopher of science, in *The Structure of Scientific Revolutions.*[2] It is associated with new discoveries in physics

---

[2] Kuhn, Thomas, *Toward a Scientific Revolution.* University of Chicago

that profoundly alter our understanding of the relationship between mind and matter. We now know that the material world is not solid, but consists of particles and waves, energies and forces. This discovery is a radical departure from the way we previously viewed the world and nature and alters the way we think. We are now developing our innate capacity to move beyond linear, sequential, and dualistic thinking to include holistic, intuitive, and unitive ways of knowing. The boundaries between matter and mind are dissolving. We now know we are an embodiment of an integration of mind, body, and spirit. Scientific and religious approaches to truth can be seen as complementary and they are gradually merging.

The rational, scientific approach is expanding to include an understanding of the value of synthetic thought, systems thinking, emotional intelligence [3] and intuition. [4] The acceptance and mastery of alternative ways of knowing has become necessary for holistic and global thinking. Dualistic thinking, which was very important in the growth of science, developed discrimination through separation and division. Unitive thinking brings synthesis to the separate parts. Unitive thinking is the type of thinking required to understand our relationship to each other and to the whole and thus to build an inclusive global civilization. Analysis of fragmented information serves to confuse rather than enlighten. Yet, it is the glue that binds the fragments that is important. Indeed, a new consciousness is arising which combines rationality, compassion, action, and a realization that we are responsible for and capable of building a new inclusive civilization based

---

Press, 1996.
[3] Goleman, Daniel, *Emotional Intelligence*. Bantam Books, 1995.
[4] Gilligan, Carol, *In a Different Voice: Psychological Theory and Women's Development*. Harvard University Press, March 1999.

on a higher consciousness and universal values.

Some External Forces of Change

Some have suggested that the main characteristic of the next century will be information. We speak about The Information Age and contrast it to the Industrial Age from which we are emerging. Exciting innovations in telecommunications are radically changing our lives. Scientific and technological innovations are making it possible to instantly connect to any part of the world we choose, at increasingly lower cost. Traditional economic theory of supply and demand is being turned upside down as telecommunication costs are *lowered* with increasing demand, making it possible for more people to participate in its benefits. When properly directed, these developments can lead to decentralization of power and democratization of knowledge.

Civil Society must engage in the technological revolution to help insure that its benefits are equally and fairly distributed. Imagine the destruction that would ensue if the Internet was controlled for selfish purposes, was used to invade privacy, or taxed so that all persons could no longer afford to use it. We must recognize and redirect negative forces that would subvert potentially positive developments for selfish purposes. We have the responsibility to keep technology democratic, transparent, and directed toward the common good. Mark Malloch Brown, Administrator of the United Nations Development Program says this:

> For many in the developing world and civil society these rapid changes are seen as a threat. Far from helping, the information explosion is seen as a major contributing factor to the growing gap between rich and poor, both within and between countries. As high technology comes to make up

an increasingly important part of the global economy, poorer countries with fewer resources and less well-educated workforces are being left further and further behind.[5]

He further describes the possible benefits that would accrue to developing countries if they were able to gain access to advanced technologies.

By eliminating space and time it gives us an unprecedented means of overcoming two of the root causes of extreme poverty—ignorance and isolation.   From dramatic improvements in distance learning to access to updated health and medical information to a newfound ability to participate in world markets, it will for the first time allow many poor and isolated groups to become part of the global community.[6]

Interconnectedness is not a new concept. The major religious traditions have taught us that each individual is a spark of the divine and all of us together make up the one humanity, the one family from One Source. Perhaps the revolution in telecommunications is a metaphor for the possibility of applying the teachings of ancient traditions to our daily lives. We need to connect not only through technology and information, but also through our hearts and souls.

We can find fault with the uncontrolled way in which some transnational corporations have exploited labor and the environment.   In this context it should be observed that grassroots groups are organizing and making progress in

---

[5] Brown, Mark Malloch, "The Internet and Development," in *Choices, The Human Development Magazine*. June 2000.
[6] *Ibid.*

preventing this exploitation. We need to support more partnering between corporations and environmental groups, so that the results of the forces of globalization will benefit all, North and South, as well as labor, management, and the environment. Business has become globalized, but the benefits have not been shared and the environment has been damaged. These discrepancies have led to grassroots protests that paralyzed the work of the World Trade Organization at its recent meeting in Seattle, USA.

We note increased mobility of people and means of receiving information. Traveling is increasing at an exponential rate, and also is immigration from developing to developed nations is intensifying. Wireless Internet and voice devices now offer the capability to be anywhere in the world and to communicate with whomever we wish. This is a positive force for change that introduces us to the cultural customs of different people, or one that conversely, can lead to intolerance. Refugees and displaced persons who can not find a home, or immigrants, who move into countries to earn a living wage or escape political persecution, are often victims of intolerance. We will need to develop much more flexibility in a mobile world.

Ethics, values and laws have not caught up with the process of globalization. A growing number of groups setting ethical standards whether in business, education, science, or sports. UNESCO's approach, *A Common Framework for Ethics in the 21st Century*[7], is a compilation of the thinking of the leading thinkers in the field of global ethics. The Universal Ethics Millennium Conference[8] is another example of the new

---

[7] *A Common Framework for Universal Ethics for the 21st Century.* Division of Philosophy and Ethics, UNESCO, Paris, 1999.

[8] Universal Ethics Millennium Forum: Final Summary. April 12, 2000.

emphasis on ethics. We can not stop the powerful forces of change, such as telecommunications, globalization, and mobility, but we can and must learn to direct these forces in a positive way for the good of all. Reevaluation of ethics and values must parallel the inner and outer forces of change.

Some Internal Forces of Change

Internal changes in consciousness and attitudes accompany external forces of change. Ken Wilber, the leading American thinker in the evolution of consciousness helps us to better understand the relationship between changes of consciousness and external forces of change[9]. He identified the relationship between patterns of growth of individuals and cultural/collective growth patterns. Through his method, he identified the most respected thinkers in the major academic disciplines, i.e. science, religion, art, psychology, anthropology, philosophy and physics. He extracted a consistent pattern, which operates through each of the separate fields of knowledge and was able to identify growth patterns in individuals and societies from both an internal and external perspective.

He traced the evolution of the collective from families to tribes, to tribal villages, to early states and empires, to nation-states, to global consciousness, our present point in history, and finally cosmic consciousness, for the committed few. He also traced the evolution of individual and cultural consciousness, that parallel collective organizational patterns. He discovered that there is a reciprocal relationship between the capacity of an individual to expand consciousness and the collective

---

[9] Wilber, Ken, *A Brief History of Everything*. Shambhalla Publications Inc., February 1996.

evolutionary changes that require new worldviews.

For example, we evolve from impulse to emotions, to symbols, concepts, and eventually to a capacity for "vision logic," or the ability to synthesize all knowledge. Our present age is moving from the Industrial Age to the Information Age. Simultaneously, we have a greater capacity for more inclusive thinking and planetary consciousness. Wilber also discovered that there is an increasing capacity to think holistically and to synthesize many diverse factors through an organizing principle that embraces and includes them all, but adds something new. We do not merely add up the different cultures and civilizations, but also discover in the process a larger organizing principle. Science and religion are both concerned with ultimate knowledge. In the new civilization there will be a much closer merging between science and religion and the evidence of this development is increasingly manifesting itself.

The next evolutionary step according to Wilber will be in a focused spiritual direction. Discipline and effort are required to reach the next evolutionary stage of consciousness, which is the development of the heart—an experienced, bonding love for all living beings. He made a clear distinction between outer forms of connection through systems theory, globalization, and knowledge and the inner experiential wisdom needed to live harmoniously with others. According to his thesis most of us are connecting globally only at the material level. A few have chosen to develop the empathic, compassionate interconnection necessary for becoming a global family. Pioneers of the global heart can be found in every culture today, dedicated to expanding consciousness to more inclusive levels. Changes of heart and mind are necessary to bring us closer to our destiny as a united humanity with diverse gifts. In the dim outlines of the new civilization, we observe the development of genuine caring and concern for other cultures and civilizations – a movement toward solidarity.

From an evolutionary perspective we discover that as the collective social world changes, new human capacities are developed to deal with the demands of the new emergence. Our own potential actually increases to meet the demands of our times.

In the old paradigm, the world was viewed primarily from a materialistic perspective. Analysis and reductionism were the most valuable tools of thought. Borders and walls were built to separate and distinguish.   It was thought that rational, sequential, and linear thinking were the only valid tools for discovering truth. In the old paradigm each person or state was considered autonomous. Therefore, a win-lose mentality arose, with self-interest paramount, and competition rampant. In a materialistic, dualistic worldview of separate, autonomous individuals and groups, scarcity and limited resources, this type of consciousness is inevitable. Competition and personal ambition lead to hierarchical structures with dominant people and civilizations positioned on top of the pyramid while the majority of humanity are at the bottom. The consequences of the "us and them" mentality and possibility of dehumanization are evidenced in wars and violence we have experienced during this period of national identification and linear, sequential thinking.

These qualities and ways of being still prevail where there is a lack of understanding that we are interconnected and are part of something larger than ourselves. As long as we resist the emerging paradigm and consider ourselves as isolated beings, autonomous and unconnected, we will unconsciously behave in a manner leading to wars and violence. With a retrogressive worldview where self-interest is primary, individually or collectively, taking care of oneself or one's community, or one's state in a world of borders, limits, separateness and scarcity, we will continue to perceive others as adversaries and dehumanize them. We will be able to commit violence without guilt. There is a reciprocal relationship between the state of the world and the evolution of consciousness. The direction of evolution today is towards less borders and more inclusiveness.

Our hearts must expand to include not just our families and communities, but all of humanity. Service to the whole becomes a prime value. In a world where the abundance of information overwhelms us, we need each other to help sort it all out. Collaboration and networking are the cultural constructs for operating successfully in the new world. Shared and rotating power is replacing individual hierarchical leaders. Facilitators who can evoke the best from members of the groups are the new leaders. Self-determination and choice is inevitable with the democratizing of information on the Internet. Our minds and hearts must go beyond our individual self-interest or that of our community to the whole world. Inclusiveness and group consciousness are the keys.

There is a strong incentive urging us to identify ourselves as planetary people. Those individuals and societies who learn to let go, reconcile, and forgive will clear their psyches for fresh and creative work on a planetary scale. Those that hold on to hatred, resentments, and revenge will learn that in addition to harming others, they also harm themselves. They may not have the inner freedom, nor the creativity to contribute to the emerging civilization.

We have always loved and served our individual communities. Today we find a growing number of sensitive pioneers of the new consciousness feeling an intense compassion for global injustices. This compassion is leading them to organize and act to rectify injustices to whomever and wherever they may occur. Individuals and groups are increasingly engaged in healing and helping people from all cultures in the world, not just their own. The Balkans Trauma Project can be seen as one example of this.[10] This expansion of consciousness includes love and a sense of responsibility for all beings, no matter where they are born, whatever their color or gender. In the new paradigm there is joy and celebration of the diversity and magnificence of our world cultures. An active international civil society is organizing. It is becoming a partner with governments and business in addressing pressing global problems, in addition to working independently at grassroots levels. However, just as the states still operate from self-interest, humanitarian organizations often also operate from self-interest or competition for funds.

Many have recognized that in order to fulfill our destiny in the new world with a positive, objective, and serene attitude, we need to practice meditation, prayer, silence, and/or turning inward for reflection. It takes a great deal of inner discipline to manage our feelings, emotions and thoughts—the dark side of pride, aggression, hate, fear, and jealousy—to move toward reconciliation and forgiveness. Self-help groups have been growing steadily since the 1960's to help one another overcome the conditioned habits of the old paradigm. Spiritual groups are proliferating as well, with motivated individuals and groups recognizing the need to change themselves in order to change the world. Alone and in groups many have helped each other to overcome dysfunctional habits through psychological groups, self-examination, meditation and acute inner

---

[10] Roof, Nancy, *The Impact of War on Humanitarian Service Providers.* Center for Psychology and Social Change, Cambridge, MA., 1994.

observation. We are not objective about our own behavior and often need feedback from others to learn where we may, unknowingly, be creating problems for others. We are still habitually conditioned in the old paradigm way of thinking, and have to be constantly alert to correct the habits that no longer serve.

The lack of recognition that we must change ourselves as well as the collective is a major deterrent to realizing the new vision and consciousness required for a new civilization. The benefit of working in groups is that we receive feedback about our unconscious patterns. There is a lack of understanding that we are creatures of developed, conditioned habits. These habitual responses continue in an automatic and repetitive manner, unless we choose to exercise a disciplined approach to change them. These conditioned habits from the old paradigm are still alive in international policy and international relations as well as in those individuals who are humanitarian servers. It is sad and frightening to witness a person in a leadership position, whether political or spiritual, self-deceived about their own human frailties, doing untold harm and damage to others, in the name of peace. We observe the faults of others long before we discover our own. Denial is the line of least resistance and is pervasive in society.

Although a strong sense of contacting the highest good within us and with others is important, it will not suffice for the work required to move into the new era. Spiritual motivation is important, but it also takes a rigorous psychological examination to root out old habits. Purifying ourselves of old paradigm reactions can be enhanced by meditations, designed to let go of the past rather than carry forward old resentments, which subtly interfere with our present service. The possibility of transcending ourselves and gaining love and support from inner resources also strengthens our ability to serve.

LEARNING TO LIVE TOGETHER

"Am I not destroying my enemies when I make them my friends?"

—Abe Lincoln

Thoughts About Differences – Dialogue Among Civilizations

President Khatami of Iran proposed a Dialogue among Civilizations at the United Nations. In September 1998 the General Assembly designated the year 2001 as the year of Dialogue among Civilizations[11]. If given enough importance this designation has potential for improving the process of international relations. A Dialogue among Civilizations has evoked much enthusiasm from several different communities, nations, groups, and individuals because of its importance and timeliness. Psychologists have long supported the view that the fundamental ingredient of any relationship, from marriage to international affairs, is the capacity to communicate and listen well. Without this foundation, relationships can easily revert to suspicion, domination, or exploitation. If a nation puts its self-interest above the interest of the other party or the whole, there is bound to be suspicion. Further, without reciprocal dialogue we make assumptions about the other's motivation, leading to distortion and misperception.

---

[11] A/RES/53/22, General Assembly, Fifty-Third Session, 16 November 1998.

Understanding differences is fundamental if we are to avert mass destruction. Transparency and openness are key in an interconnected world. Secrecy leads to suspicion and manipulation. Old paradigm thinking is based on the erroneous perception that we are separate and isolated, and therefore self-interest becomes the primary value. In the new paradigm when everything from science to trends in globalization has resulted in a new worldview, the need for dialogue in the spirit of understanding between states could not be more timely.

Mr. Hadi Nejad Hosseinain, Ambassador and Permanent Representative of the Islamic Republic of Iran to the United Nations, described the old paradigm way of conducting international relations and the possibility of a new approach as follows:

> Representatives of governments customarily enter a political negotiation process with elaborate strategy and tactic to prevail, achieve a predetermined objective and secure their national interests to the largest possible extent among civilizations... Hopefully, in a dialogue among peoples of various civilizations...would also have a strategy and tactic, not to prevail and overcome the other party or parties, but to listen, to hear, to comprehend, to share and then try to accommodate the concerns, the fears and the preoccupations of the other party in order to enhance mutual understanding...[12]

The article will now explore some thoughts about dialogue itself. First, it offers a context and a definition of dialogue, with a rationale for its timely importance, followed by some

---

[12] Dialogue Among Civilizations: Call for Common Ground. Panel Discussion at the United Nations.

observations about the dynamics of dialogue. Moreover, the article will discuss the need for full engagement, reciprocal respect as equals, the skills involved in listening, and finally some thoughts about inner dialogue. Because of its overriding importance, a separate section is reserved to discuss the effect of operating from different levels of values and worldviews within and between cultures.

Mr. Hadi Nejad Hosseinain, placed the Dialogue Among Civilizations in the current context of globalization.

> Therefore, the delicate balance in a globalized world is how to celebrate each and every culture and civilization and allow each to make its contribution to the fullest of its potential to the ultimate shape of our world. Globalization must prove to be an ultimate complete whole, but at the same time, and in reality, made up of many smaller ingredients that are each a living culture with different shade which work together in a mutually enriching and reinforcing process.[13]

Dr. M. Javad Faridzadeh, President of the International Center of Dialogue among Civilizations, expanded upon the crucial importance of dialogue:

> The act of dialogue comprises the purest human deed and is even coextensive with the sum and substance and the true essence of being human. Through dialogue human beings get to open windows unto each other's existence and through such openings deeper levels of existence are brought to the fore in both parties to the dialogue. When dialogue is instituted between cultures or civilizations, the existential depth and scope of both parties widens

---

[13] *Ibid.*

accordingly. Moreover, a dialogue among civilizations fosters understanding among various parties, and understanding antecedes peace and friendship.[14]

At the same panel discussion, Dialogue Among Civilizations: A Call for Common Ground, Dr. Faridzadeh presented a definition of dialogue, its purpose and ultimate aim.

By dialogue we specifically mean well-defined rational and ethical endeavors to gain knowledge about the other cultural and civilization domains with the ultimate aim of engaging in empathic and compassionate discourse with them.[15]

This definition emphasizes the new approach of both rationality and compassion, or head and heart, and serves to define dialogue at a deeper level than conversation or exchange of information.

At the conference the speakers stressed the need for an inter-disciplinary approach to dialogue. The insights from Educational Psychology were one of the areas indicated as important for understanding the full dimensions of dialogue. Psychologists have researched the art of communication and dialogue in individual and social situations, and can offer decades of research and practical experience. Some suggestions from psychology for meaningful dialogue follow.

One important insight involves the depth of authentic dialogue. Students of human nature are aware of an innate feeling that evaluates whether or not a speaker is fully engaged in what they are articulating. If they are merely conveying

---

[14] *Ibid.*
[15] *Ibid.*

information, without feeling and emotion, we know that there will be no true understanding between speaker and listener. The speaker is not fully present to the listener. In larger meetings when somebody reads a paper rather than makes contact with the audience, we find ourselves yawning with boredom and unable to fully remember the content. We know the speaker is not in dialogue with us, but with him/herself. It takes the full presence of a person to engage in authentic dialogue. The tonal quality and body language with which it is delivered tell us a great deal about whether we are passive recipients of a separative monologue or whether we are engaged in an authentic unitive and interconnecting dialogue.

Respect is essential for effective dialogue. Dialogue is a reciprocal and mutual process between equals. If one side is attempting to impose its own ideas there is no dialogue because the old paradigm thinking will be dominant, dividing the parties into a dualistic dynamic. In effective dialogue both parties are engaged in a unified process of teaching and learning from each other to the immense benefit of both.

Dialogue requires the capacity to listen. The art of listening is something that does not come easily to most people. Therefore, training groups are sometimes needed to help gain awareness of when and how we are listening. The primary problem is that there is a tendency to be thinking about what to say next, rather than to fully listen to the speaker. There is no true absorption of what the speaker is saying because the listener is not acknowledging what is heard, but is rehearsing his/her own reactions and responses. This type of exchange becomes a monologue between two isolated parties, and is of no benefit to either. When civilization and states are engaged in international relations these principles apply as well. How many interactions between states are authentic dialogues? Increased awareness about engaging reciprocally in dialogue can result in vastly improved relationships at all levels.

The value of listening cannot be underestimated if the goal is to learn about other cultures and civilizations. We might say it is a fundamental skill needed for individual and global peace. We are all conditioned by our cultural backgrounds. There is a psychological tendency to assume what is normal for us is also normal for others. At the United Nations, where all cultures and civilizations of the world meet, we find that there are many different perspectives on any global issue, and that our own is only one of them. We require dialogue, rather than assumptions in order to avoid cultural misunderstandings.

Lastly, it is a fact of the human condition that we live in two worlds—the inner and outer. Just as there is dialogue between individuals, groups, and countries, we constantly have inner conversations with different parts of ourselves. Unless one has practiced self-observation, most people are not aware of the negative and positive comments that are directing us from inside. We often have inner dialogues between two conflicting parts of ourselves, but are unaware of the effect these have on our outer relationships. We can all begin with ourselves in learning to listen inside to whether we are dominating, submitting, criticizing, open, transparent, or accepting. By self-observation we discover the intensity and tonal quality indicative of our real motivation. More importantly, we discover we may be reacting out of old habitual conditioning from the old paradigm. Nevertheless, we can choose to change, rather than to react automatically, by gaining mastery over our minds through self-observation and meditation.

Relationship between Values and Levels of Consciousness

The preceding part of this article underlined the discussion at the United Nations regarding Dialogue among Civilizations. This dialogue, however, examined the cultures and civilizational aspect, but neglected the psychological and spiritual dimensions. Conflicts arise also because of different levels of needs and development leading to different beliefs, values and worldviews operating within and between cultures.

Differences in values and ethics are directly related to the way we experience life and our resulting worldview. For example, when we view life from a limited perspective, based on the need to survive, our values are driven by fear, leading to hostility, greed, possessiveness, and lack of trust. When our need is primarily for self esteem, we are driven by ambition and status needs. When, however, we grow beyond the need for self esteem we relate to the world with openness, a sense of security and interconnectedness. It is only at this stage of development that our highest values and ethics drive our behavior.

Several psychologists and religious traditions trace the levels of development of the - individual, including, Ken Wilber's work on levels of individual and collective consciousness and Abraham Maslow work on the hierarchy of needs which demonstrates levels of individual growth. [16] Religions, in particular Buddhism, teach the possible levels from which the human can operate, from the gross to subtle. A crucial element of successful dialogue is to recognize from what primary need or value the other person or country is operating. Developing countries have different needs from developed countries, just as individuals differ in their development. Further, Richard Barrett has discovered that

---

[16] Maslow, Abraham, *Toward a Psychology and Being*. Wiley and Sons, November 1998.

different styles of leadership are appropriate for different stages of development.[17]

His levels, based on the primary identification of the individual or group are:

- Levels of Needs and Values -

Primary Identification	Appropriate Style of Leadership
1) survival	1) authoritarian
2) relationship	2) paternalistic
3) self-esteem	3) hierarchical
4) transformation	4) team building
5) meaning	5) collaborative
6) making a difference	6) partnering, mentoring
7) service	7) visionary

He begins with the primary need for instinctual survival. Authoritarian leadership is appropriate for this stage. Next, relationship becomes the prime value, where we focus on the need to belong. A paternalistic leadership style is appropriate for this stage. Next is the need for self-esteem, where the primary focus is ambition, self-respect, and success. The correlating leadership style is some form of hierarchical structure. A high value would be placed on being the leader *over* other people. At the fourth, or transformational level, a major shift begins to happen in one's values and worldview.

---

[17] Barrett, Richard, *Liberating the Corporate Soul: Building a Visionary Organization*. Butterworth-Heinemann, October 1998.

Often a crisis precedes this stage, when personal growth and understanding become the primary identification. Leadership is needed that facilitates human interaction, participation, and team building. In most development systems we move through physical, emotional, and mental levels on our way to spiritual development. In Barrett's system level 5 identifies the primary value as finding meaning. Self-interest is losing its power. Collaborative leadership is appropriate for this stage. Level 6 puts a high value on making a difference and a sense of social responsibility, rather than personal fulfillment. Leaders become partners, mentors, or coaches at this stage. Finally, his most inclusive value is service to the whole. The type of leadership appropriate to this stage would be visionary.

What is the value of understanding a hierarchy of needs and values? Just imagine a person or country at a survival level, trying to establish a collaborative form of leadership. When safety or survival is an issue all the higher values can disappear. An authoritarian approach is often best during chaotic periods. Imagine trying to speak about the common good with someone who is driven by ambition and the primary need to be important and win. When the whole spectrum of values and worldviews is studied, it becomes clear that the nature of differences is more than differences in cultures. At the top of the hierarchy, the capacity to understand and value the common good is what gives meaning to life. These values are evidenced within all cultures and civilizations. It is because there are individuals who do operate from these higher ethical and moral perspectives that we have hope for the world. Understanding the different levels on which we ourselves are capable of operating is indispensable self-knowledge. It is indispensable knowledge for dialoguing with others as well. Individuals from different cultures or civilizations who are operating with similar values and worldviews often have more in common than with members of their own culture who operate from a different value system.

Those who operate from the world service perspective need to understand that their values are not those that generally operate in the real world. Those with serious idealistic leanings have often been faulted for not recognizing that many people in the world are not interested in ethics and morality. Most individuals and groups are driven by survival, belonging and closeness, or self-esteem needs and thus ambition, status and power over others is the motivating force rather than genuine dialogue. Many are still operating from old paradigm values. Inherent differences of worldviews and values must be recognized and dealt with, if we are to have substantive dialogue rather than idealistic or unrealistic hopes.

Thoughts about Commonalties—Spirituality

In preparing ourselves for the new civilization we learn to honor our diversity and uniqueness as well as to recognize and honor our commonalties. All components of reality are comprised of parts within wholes, whether we refer to matter, mind, or life. For example, a whole atom is part of a whole molecule, the molecule part of a cell, the cell part of an organism etc. We belong to families, communities, nations and the planet—parts within wholes, ad infinitum. The task of the part is to become autonomous while communicating with other equal parts. The part must also find its place in the larger whole to which it belongs. Each part has the capacity to transcend itself as well as destroy itself. In the international community states examine the notion of sovereignty and international relations, but fail to consider the larger context, the whole.

The task is to harmonize these often conflicting basic

needs. Traditional psychology addresses the task of the part, which is to develop autonomy and individuality. It also addresses relationships between individuals and groups, including international relations. Transpersonal Psychology and the ageless wisdom of all religious traditions address the larger whole to which the parts belong. Religious traditions have taught that we are divine sparks of a larger whole, regardless of whether we call it an Energy, a Force, the One Source, Buddha-nature, or God. Spiritual disciplines help us to transcend the part's concerns with bruised egos, pride, and fear, and become secure in our common identification with a larger whole.

Inter-religious dialogue and dialogue among civilizations, in this context, can promote the interconnectedness between diverse elements. However, to play a full role, they must transcend their framework and connect to a holistic organizing principle that embraces them all.

From the perspective of this article, spirituality does not exclusively refer to religion, but connotes a universal principle that transcends them all. It is something inherent within that believes in goodness, truth and beauty, right human relations, and love. It uplifts and elevates all we do for the highest good. The spiritual part of all individuals wants to contribute to making the world a better place to live in, whether that is in the field of science, education, religion, finance, government, or the social sciences. It is that inner urge to be the very best person we can be under all circumstances of life. All people have this innate sense of goodness at some deep level. In the new civilization people will increasingly act out of this higher self. Some already are making the commitment to undertake this change in inner being in addition to focussing on outer changes.

A commitment to the common good addresses the needs of the vulnerable and marginalized.   Self-sacrifice, service, purifying our own inner thoughts and emotions, reflecting on the common good, and developing right human relations for the good of the collective are the values we live by. We would change our values from those of competition, winning, and gaining material wealth and power, to the common good.

Momentum is building in the international community to incorporate ethics, values, and spirituality as a crosscutting approach to global issues.   In discussions on dialogue among civilizations, states have begun to talk about the ethics of international relations. Harold H. Saunders, who served five American Presidents in the National Security Council and Department of State   recommends that international relations emphasize the *relationship* between nations. [18] There is a growing number of discussion groups forming to view global problems from ethical and values perspectives.   The Values Caucus has initiated several forums with Ambassadors and key persons in the UN Secretariat in New York, based on a value or ethical perspective.   Viewing poverty, for example, within an ethical context, helps us re-frame our approach and motivate responsibility and action to overcome this totally unacceptable condition.   Secretary General Kofi Annan has called for The Millennium World Peace Summit of Religious and Spiritual Leaders in August 2000.

Global standards at the United Nations are incorporated in various documents such as the United Nations Charter and the Declaration of Human Rights. However, the Declaration has been criticized as weighted in favor of Western values. A more

---

[18] Saunders, Harold, "An Historic Challenge to Rethink How Nations Relate," in *The Psychodynamics of International Relations*. Lexington Books, 1990.

recent document is the Earth Charter, which took nine years of effort to write and used an innovative process that maximized global participation. Efforts are being made to humanize globalization. In particular, the *Human Development Report* addresses the quality of life as well as the material aspects. The report *Our Global Neighborhood*[19] expresses the role of values in global issues and *Response to Our Global Neighborhood*[20] adds more to the theme. More recently the General Assembly designation of the year of Dialogue among Civilizations and UNESCO's Common Framework for Universal Values in the 21st Century, advocate value-centered approaches to globalization. The Universal Ethics Millenium Conference is another NGO contribution aimed at drawing attention to the importance of ethics and values in international affairs. The United Nations is viewed by many as the global center of our planet, where all nations, cultures and civilizations work together for world peace and progress.

Several groups exist at the present time that are inspired and committed to the spiritual task of meditating for global peace. They include members of the UN Secretariat and the diplomatic community. It is remarkable how many members of the NGO community have given up lucrative incomes and successful careers to voluntarily use their skills to build an international civil society for a better world. When we meet and work with dedicated and unselfish servers, our hope for humanity is renewed. We celebrate with joy that we are alive today in a time of such immense possibility.

---

[19] *Our Global Neighborhood,* Report of the Commission on Global Governance, Oxford University Press, 1995.

[20] *A People's Response to Our Global Neighborhood,* Boston Research Center for the 21st Century, 1995.

TOWARDS A NEW CIVILIZATION

We don't so much solve problems as we outgrow them

Carl Jung

Individual and Collective Approaches

Increasing numbers of people have understood the nature of our transitional times. Some have chosen to begin the process of change individually, following the old maxim "Let there be peace and let it begin with me." Others have chosen to begin with the collective, directly addressing community and global issues such as peace and security, disarmament, poverty, human rights, violence, and sustainable development. There is a need to find new approaches and methods to develop our individual potential and to find creative means and new ways to solve our collective problems. Both individual and collective approaches are needed.

Those working on the mastery of the inner world, through psychological or spiritual means eventually realize that this approach is necessary, but not sufficient. Psychologically and spiritually we need to master our inner impulses, minds and emotions, and develop a connection with the source of our being. This inner mastery is essential to peace and serenity. However, social, economic, and global problems intimately affect our individual lives as well. For example, untreated trauma resulting from violence can break down all efforts to behave in a loving and objective manner. Trauma leaves us in a dehumanized condition, without feelings, and with a propensity to harm others. As humans we are simply unable to contain the horror of acts of savagery. Despite our good intentions, we become less able to live our most cherished values and spiritual commitments. Intense stress from our collective environment, at any level, affects our capacity for objectivity and emotional control.

Those who begin with collective problems, soon discover that offering to engage in public service is necessary, but not sufficient. They discover that despite good intentions, good human relations with colleagues, groups, and nations often break down. Most people believe that they are acting from good intentions, despite the harm that may befall others because of their behavior. Psychologically, humans have a high capacity for denial about their own intentions and the results of their actions. Humanitarian and international leaders will eventually realize that inner peace and security are of equal importance to outer peace and security. As they interact in their work, they will also realize the importance of inter-relational skills gained through understanding organizational development, group dynamics, and conflict management with peers and authorities.

Components of a New Civilization

In a new civilization there will be understanding and honoring of diverse cultures and civilizations. Tolerating others is not enough to heal the wounds in the world. Each culture and civilization will be honored for the contribution it makes to the whole. There is celebration of our diversity. As we welcome our surface differences and explore our deeper essences, we learn that our commonalities outweigh our differences. In the new civilization we will learn that we are our brother's keeper.

At this juncture of time in history we contemplate the biggest challenges we face in saving our planet and ourselves from destruction and building together a harmonious and interconnected world. What are the values that are most important to us, standing on the brink of a new era sharing our home, the planet Earth, connected by webs and networks? Values evolve. We have outgrown many practices, which were acceptable in the past, such as slavery, colonialism, the inferiority of women, and many more. What kind of values will be the foundation for a planetary civilization? Many of the ancient values of humanity remain the same. The Golden Rule, do unto others as you would have them do unto you, is taught in some form, in all major religious and ethical traditions. Today we must apply our values to a larger context. It is not only in our immediate community, or nation that we practice the Golden Rule, but also to every man, woman, and child in the world, in every culture and every civilization, and for the sake of future generations. What is new? It is an enlarged context within which to practice our ancient values.

Building solidarity is another challenge, which involves a much larger context than in the past. Now we must care for and be concerned for all of humanity. Social responsibility becomes global responsibility. Building solidarity involves the heart, not merely a connected world, but one that cares. At the United Nations, several NGO projects provide humanitarian aid to diverse cultures and civilizations. When famines occur, aid comes forth from all over the world. But it is a difficult matter to build caring and concerned compassion for all living beings as well as for future generations. Yet, according to Ken Wilber, we can expect to mature into an expanded heart connection that the religions have taught was our true destiny. The expanded mass media and Internet can help by objectively informing us of what is going on in the world and where our help is needed. Building solidarity requires growing beyond our cultural differences and identifying and caring for all members of the human race.

Self-determination and empowerment are key ideas in the

psychological history of humanity. Current trends are moving in the direction of decentralization of authority and increasing self-determination from relationships with our doctors, dentists, and financial advisors, to democratic governments. A key component has been the decentralization and democratization of the individual and collective through the World Wide Web. Transparency and availability of information continue to bring radical changes in the locus of power.

New movements in spirituality are supporting engagement in the world, in addition to traditional practices such as meditation and prayer. Now more than ever, there is a drive to understand, love, and take action on the values that are important for collective society. International civil society has been building rapidly since the United Nations conducted major international conferences on the rights of the child, sustainable development, women, population, social development, human rights, and habitat. The recognition that action and organization were needed to take responsibility for the direction of our common future emerged with thousands of participants and increasing numbers of international organizations. The large international conference called The Hague Appeal for Peace in 1999 was sponsored by international civil society. In May 2000 the first Millenium Forum took place, where international civil society addressed the key United Nations issues. Civil society is now being recognized as a necessary partner with governments at the United Nations.

More people are identifying themselves as world or planetary citizens. They are learning how to become an effective voice in determining the future of the planet. They want to be involved in decisions that ultimately affect their lives. They are taking advantage of courses in organizational development and teamwork to increase their effectiveness.

The power of the People acting in unison has resulted in a global standard on the elimination of landmines. The movement for an International Criminal Court was another successful global movement initiated by grassroots efforts. More recently, action to protest the World Trade Organization was effective in slowing down the process, in order to force a reevaluation of the benefits of globalization and the effect on the environment. The power of the people to facilitate significant worldwide changes is now apparent.

Inner peace, the field of psychology and religion, is now recognized by many as essential to living a well-balanced and effective life. Many are seeking solitude and retreats as a restorative process to balance outer service. Much more time is spent discovering who we are and developing disciplines and methods of obtaining inner peace. A high value is placed on inner peace and the effect it has on the way we act in the outer world.

We are learning to share leadership and work together through networks. Shaping our own destiny and being a part of decisions that affect us have become critically important. The old paternalism and authority patterns of the past are beginning to be replaced by newer methods of shared power and resources.

The essential challenge we face as we move into a radically different world is the clash of values with those who still hold on to the values, ways of living, and institutions of the old paradigm. Those who gained power through these values often find it extremely difficult to give up the power they have achieved and accept the shared leadership style appropriate for our age. When a value has become a prevailing standard and considered normal, it is much more difficult to change, especially when it has become institutionalized in our governments, religious institutions, schools, and medicine. We must reevaluate all our institutions and values to realign them with the sweeping advances of evolution.

Self-esteem in the past was often built on hierarchical power and some form of domination. In the new era, self-esteem will come from building networks of shared power. In the old we feared failure, and dependency—we suffered from foolish pride, greed, and the inability to escape from hatred and revenge. Can we build a new world where we can learn to overcome these difficult human deficits, which have so cruelly dominated our inner lives and our relations with others? It is a long and difficult struggle. Our hope is high because many individuals are determined to face reality individually and collectively with all our human foibles and rise up to celebrate life and each other.

CONCLUSION

We are in a transitional period between two paradigms. Our knowledge of the fundamental nature of reality has changed radically. In the old view we perceived matter as solid, and ourselves as separate from others. Today, we know what appears as solid matter consists of waves and particles. We are all connected through a network of webs in both the inner and outer life. However, habits, attitudes, and reactions are difficult to change. To change the world we must change ourselves, our relations with others, our institutions, international relations and our connection to a larger whole that embraces all. We must envision a new world based on the fundamental reality of our interconnectedness rather than conditioned habits of separateness, which hinder creativity. We are responsible for the way we leave this planet to the next generations. We all have a part to play in envisioning and building a future we can be proud of. We need the courage to face our personal weaknesses and strengths and to understand the fragile world we live in, so that our service will be constructive in all respects, and that we can live and act according to our highest values.

A MORE HUMANE WORLD ORDER :
TOWARDS A NEW CIVILIZATION

Patricia M. Mische, Ed.D.

Dr. Patricia M. Mische is Lloyd Professor of Peace Studies and World Law at Antioch College. She is co-founder and President Emerita of Global Education Associates and the author of many books and articles, including *Toward a Human World Order: Beyond the National Security Straightjacket* (with Gerald Mische). She teaches in the Peace Education Program at Columbia University, and has given more than 1000 workshops and courses at universities around the world. She has received numerous awards recognizing her work in global education and international development.

In the modern world, religion is a central, perhaps the central, force that motivates and mobilizes people. It is sheer hubris to think that because Soviet communism has collapsed, the West has won the world for all time and that Muslims, Chinese, Indians, and others are going to rush to embrace Western liberalism as the only alternative. The Cold War division of humanity is over. The more fundamental divisions of humanity in terms of ethnicity, religions, and civilizations remain and spawn new conflicts.

Samuel P. Huntington

The Clash of Civilizations and the Remaking of World Order. 1996

The world is in the process of going through a revolution. Under our eyes in our lifetime we are seeing an old world dissolving and a new world coming into existence; and this great secular revolution, through which we feel ourselves to be passing, seems likely to produce a revolution in the relations between the religions.

Arnold Toynbee

"What are the Characteristics of the Contemporary World?" 1957

In his famous, if controversial, book, *The Clash of Civilizations and_the Remaking of World Order*, Samuel Huntington asserted that, contrary to common expectations, the end of the Cold War had not led to a more harmonious world order and end to global conflict. Tensions between the superpowers had declined, but in their place the world would increasingly be challenged by conflicts and wars between diverse cultural, ethnic and religious groups in a "clash of civilizations."

Huntington repudiated the "end of history" thesis of Francis Fukuyama who had written: "We may be witnessing the end of history as such: that is, the end point of mankind's ideological evolution and the universalization of Western liberal democracy as the final form of government." Huntington argued that rather than gaining power; the West was actually declining in relative influence in the world in the face of a new balance of power that was emerging in global politics. This new balance of power was not bipolar, nor unipolar under the remaining superpower, but multi-polar and multi-civilizational. The most important distinctions between peoples are now not ideological, political, or economic, but cultural, he asserted; and the most important groupings of states and conflict formation will no longer be the three blocs of the Cold War, but rather the world's seven or eight major civilizations. Huntington predicted that the future would be riddled with conflict between these clashing civilizations. "Culture and cultural identities, which at the broadest level are civilization identities, are shaping the patterns of cohesion, disintegration, and conflict in the post-Cold-War world." Huntington referred to the actors in this new world order as "The West and the rest," and urged Westerners to defend their own survival by reaffirming and preserving their Western identity against "challenges from non-Western societies." And, to avoid a global war of civilizations he urged world leaders to accept and cooperate to maintain the multi-civilizational character of global politics.

RELIGION AS A CENTRAL FORCE IN CIVILIZATIONS

Religion will be "a central force—perhaps the central force"—that motivates and mobilizes people in this civilization-based world order, Huntington said.

The importance of religion as a central force in cultures and civilizations was underscored four decades earlier by the eminent historian Arnold Toynbee, whose work Huntington sometimes cites. However, in contrast to Huntington, Toynbee was less concerned about the clashes between civilizations or religions, and more interested in the dynamic role religion and spirituality played in the inner life of civilizations, including their birth and death. Most civilizations did not die from clashes with outside forces, said Toynbee. Rather, they died of suicide. They died by severing themselves from their spiritual core.

From his comprehensive study of the rise and fall of all the major civilizations in history, Toynbee concluded that in all spirituality had served as a chrysalis from which they grew. Between the death of one civilization and the rise of a new one were creative minorities who, with deep spiritual vision or religious motivation, served to birth a new civilization from the ashes of the old one. This spiritual core was vital to a civilization's ability to sustain itself. Civilizations that lost their spiritual core soon fell into decline. Thus, unlike many historians who saw the forces of spirituality or religion as minor if interesting notes in history, or who examined religious history as a subtopic of history, Toynbee became convinced that spiritual development and religion were the alpha and omega of history. Human history was "a vision of God's creation on the move, from God its source toward God its goal."[1] Religions were not the handmaids of civilizations; rather, civilizations were the handmaids of religion, asserted Toynbee. We have civilizations in order that we may have higher religions.[2] The end or aim of human history is spiritual development—greater consciousness of and closeness to the sacred source.

Like Huntington, Toynbee prophesied a decline of Western civilization and influence in the face of counter-forces, but unlike Huntington, Toynbee was not as concerned about the long-range preservation of Western civilization. He accepted that civilizations are finite, not infinite, and that Western civilization, like others before it, would fade away, and another civilization would emerge in its place. Whereas Huntington rejected the notion that we were moving toward a universal civilization, Toynbee asserted that that is exactly where history is headed.

Of course, in this, Toynbee was taking a longer-range view of history—to be precise, a four thousand year view. Writing in 1947, he projected a trajectory of the future from 2047 to 5047. To the question: "What will historians say in 2047?" he answered: "The great event of the twentieth century was the impact of Western civilization upon all the other living societies of that day." One thousand years later, however, in the year 3047, Western civilization would have been transformed "by a counter-radiation of influences from foreign worlds which we, in our day, are in the act of engulfing in

---

[1] *A Study of History*, X, 1954, 3.
[2] *Ibid*, VII, 1954, 444.

ours." By 4047 historians would look back on developments leading up to the unification of humanity. By then, the parochial heritage will have been "battered to bits by the collision with other parochial heritages," and from this wreckage a new common life will emerge. Finally, in the year 5047 the historian will say that "the importance of this social unification of [hu]mankind was not to be found in the field of technics and economics, not in the field of war and politics, but in the field of religion."[3]

To assert that there is a vital relationship between religion and civilization is not to assert that they are synonymous. Distinctions between them should not be blurred. While religion influences and to a certain degree may affect the culture and shape of a civilization, it is not the same as a civilization. Toynbee advised Western Christians to separate their religious and spiritual heritage from Western civilization. Christianity did not originate in the West, but predated Western civilization. It became a midwife for the development of Western civilization, yet was never a monopoly of the West. From its early history, when Christianity spread around the Mediterranean and to parts of Asia, Africa and Europe, its members included people from many diverse cultures and civilizations. Moreover, Toynbee believes that Christianity would outlive Western civilization, continuing to be a spiritual force thousands of years after Western civilization had passed away. Toynbee also cautioned that there are elements in Western civilization that were not Christian, and some that were de-Christianized over time. For example, the Western tradition of politics and war are not Christian in origin. Christianity grew up under Roman rule, and its members were marginalized within the Roman Empire. They had no political

---

[3] *Ibid,* XII 595-98.

power, nor were they, by the tenets of their faith, to participate in military service.[4] In contrast, Western civilization under the Greeks and Romans, and today, has a high commitment to political and military power.

Similarly, some other religions should not be made synonymous with, or over-identified with, one civilization. Today, the major world religions have adherents from many diverse cultures and civilizations and from diverse races and ethnic groups. These religions are global communities in microcosm.   Their networks and activities bridge many cultures.

One of Toynbee's major concerns about Western civilization was that it was losing its spiritual core. "Authentic" religion was being supplanted by ungrounded faith in modern ideologies such as nationalism, communism, or in science and technology.   He considered these to be "false" religions because instead of a higher spiritual power they "worshipped man" and "collective human power." Toynbee warned against state idolatry and considered both nationalism and communism to be forms of worshipping collective human power.

Wars of religion did concern Toynbee, not only because of the senseless loss of life and displacement of people during the time of the war, but also because wars demeaned and undermined true religion, with profound and far-reaching consequences for future history.   For example, the Wars of Religion in the West, which were waged from the 13th century onward for some four hundred years, were a very militant chapter in the history of the Christian Church of the West, and, although this period may now seem ancient history and remote from people of today, the forces it unleashed, and the reaction

---

[4] *Christianity Among the Religions of the World*, 1957, 62-67.

to them, are still active forces today. Not only did these wars fracture Western Christians into hostile groups and cause displaced Europeans of different Christian denominations to flow to the Americas where they constructed a new political map around religious and anti-religious divisions, but it also filled many people with a horror or distrust of religion. In reaction there followed the secularization of the West, the "transfer of spiritual treasure" to the promotion of science and technology, and ultimately a misplaced faith in collective human power. [5] In turn, this misplaced faith in, and competition over, collective human power, fed political, social, economic and military dynamics that spiraled into the development of atomic weapons and the threat of mutually assured destruction.

Religious dialogue is key to overcoming these false gods and putting history on its true course, according to Toynbee. He called on religions not to drop their religious convictions, but to let go of their rivalries and hostilities and to seek common ground. He suggested that the common ground they needed was already available in: 1) human nature (all religions are concerned with overcoming human self-centeredness—his definition of original sin); 2) the present state of the world (modern technology had unified the world to a certain extent by "annihilating distance": problems that were previously local had now become global; all the world's religions are now confronted by a set of common problems; "We are all now one another's keepers," he wrote); [6] 3) the fact that all higher religions share a conviction that humans are "not the greatest spiritual presence in the Universe, but that there is a greater presence—God or absolute reality—and that the true end of

[5] *Ibid*, 75-79.
[6] *Ibid*, 87.

[humans] is to place [themselves] in harmony with this"; and 4) the fact that all have a common adversary in the modern "worship of man" and "collective human power." "By comparison with this fundamental issue on which all the living higher religions find themselves on the same side, the issues that divide them seem secondary. In these grave circumstances, ought we not to consider whether the higher religions should not subordinate their differences with one another and stand together against their common adversary?"[7]

In advocating inter-religious dialogue, Toynbee was not advocating syncretism—the construction of an artificial religion from elements from all the religions. Inter-religious dialogue does not mean abandoning one's beliefs or spiritual path; but it may help to deepen it, said Toynbee. One can hold fast to one's own ideals and essential truths without succumbing to fanaticism, arrogance or self-centeredness. By learning to respect, revere, admire and love each other's faiths, inter-religious dialogue helps us make progress in our own. He saw inter-religious dialogue as the antidote to religious suppression and a path to greater spiritual maturity in history. To suppress a rival religion is not an answer to our great problems of the day, said Toynbee; in the end it leads to spiritual impoverishment. He relates the lament of Quintus Aurelius Symmachus, the spokesman for the Roman Senate when the Christian Roman imperial government forced the close of pagan Roman temples: "It is impossible that so great a mystery should be approached by one road only."[8]

The mystery of which Symmachus spoke—the mystery of a greater spirit and power in the universe and in human life—is

---

[7] *Ibid*, 81.
[8] *Ibid*, 112.

still alive and seeking expression in the world today. Inter-religious dialogue may indeed be a key to opening the door to greater peace and a more humane world order in the 21st century.

RELIGIOUS IDENTIFICATION AND INTER-RELIGIOUS DIALOGUE

Toynbee was much respected as a scholar and historian, but was also criticized by some fellow historians for what they considered his over-emphasis on religion. Instead of relenting, he intensified his scholarship and, based on further findings, took even stronger positions in this area. Huntington, too, has been criticized for assigning such a significant role to religion. Although one may question some of these authors' assumptions and assertions, it is hard to dismiss entirely the view that religion will be a significant factor in the world of the 21st century.

Trends show that religious identification around the world has been growing and will continue to increase. Those identifying themselves as Christians were numbered at close to 2 billion in 1998 and are expected to reach 2.25 billion by 2025. Muslims, at close to 1.8 billion in 1998, will reach 1.96 billion by 2025. Hindus will increase from 767 million to more than 1 billion. Though with lesser numbers, Buddhists, Sikhs, Jews, and those identifying with tribal religions are also expected to increase steadily. In contrast, those identifying themselves as atheist numbered only 146 million in 1998, and are expected to increase only slightly to 152 million.[9] While population growth

---

[9] *International Bulletin of Missionary Research*, January 1998, Religion News Service.

(being born into a religious identification) will account for some of the increase, it does not account for all of it. Interest in religion is growing in many world regions among people who did not previously consider themselves religious.

There has also been a growing trend in inter-religious dialogue. The 20th century may have been a century of terrible wars, including genocide and ethnic cleansing committed or tolerated in the name of religion, but it was also a century that, perhaps as a reaction to those wars and an effort to prevent more conflict, saw unprecedented growth in inter-religious dialogue. It also gave rise to many multi-religious organizations to facilitate such dialogue, including such groups as the International Association for Religious Freedom, the Fellowship of Reconciliation, the World Conference on Religion and Peace, the Council for a Parliament for World Religions, the World Council of Churches, the Council of Christians and Jews, the United Religions Initiative, the series of inter-religious dialogues on The Contribution by Religions to the Culture of Peace sponsored by the UN Educational, Scientific and Cultural Organization (UNESCO), and many more.   This suggests growing interest in the potential of religion to be a force not only of clashes and conflicts, but also to prevent clashes, resolve conflicts, and contribute to a more humane world order for the 21st century.

Up to now, inter-religious dialogue has focused primarily on developing greater peace and understanding between people from diverse religious traditions, and also, in some cases, on promoting values of peace, social justice, human rights, and ecological integrity. There has not been that much focus on the contribution of religions to the development of a more humane world order or more just global systems and forms of governance. In a period of increasing globalization, such a focus becomes ever more urgent.

GLOBAL TRANSFORMATION: BREAKDOWN AND BREAKTHROUGH

Global Education Associates (GEA) was founded by Gerald Mische and myself to, in part, focus on the linkages between religion and world order, and since its founding in 1973, has sponsored a series of multi-religious symposia on this theme, often with the co-sponsorship or partnership of religious and multi-religious organizations around the world. The process explored in this symposium series began with a perception that we live in a time of profound, global-scale transformation. Earlier views on the nature and scope of this transformation, and the problems and opportunities emanating from it, were shared by Gerald Mische and me in our 1977 book, *Toward a Human World Order: Beyond the National Security Straitjacket.*[10] This work included an analysis of the constraints on full human development imposed by existing world systems, and called for cross-cultural dialogue and cooperative initiatives to advance more humane global systems based on core human values and an ethic of global responsibility. It included a chapter on Religion and World Order that was the fruit of our inter-religious dialogues up to that time. The fruit of some of the subsequent dialogues in the series were shared in GEA publications, including *The Whole Earth Papers*, and *Breakthrough*, and in the journals of some of GEA's partners in various symposia that were part of this process.

---

[10] Gerald and Patricia Mische, *Toward a Human World Order: Beyond the National Security Straitjacket*, Paulist Press, 1977.

From our experience with local communities in Africa, Latin America, and Asia, Gerald Mische and I had seen firsthand how, by the early 1970s, rampant global economic forces were wreaking havoc on local communities and their goals for full human development. It was from a concern for local cultures and communities that we first founded Global Education Associates as a forum for multicultural dialogue on world order and alternative futures. With Margaret Mead, the first contributor to GEA, we believed that one should "never doubt that a small group of thoughtful, committed citizens can change the world. Indeed it is the only thing that ever has." The number of GEA associates around the world soon grew to include men and women in 90 countries and more than 150 partner organizations, affiliates and collaborating networks.

The signs of transformation we saw then, which became even more pronounced over the next decades, included symptoms of breakdown at every level of life—political, economic, cultural, ecological, and spiritual. Old systems that had been created to serve the needs of traditional civilizations of the past, and the state-centric system of the modern world, could no longer respond effectively to the new challenges presented by rapid globalization and increasing global interdependence. And new systems capable of meeting these challenges humanely and effectively had yet to be created.

We described this time/space as a certain "between time"—a parenthesis between one age that was dying (this was well before the end of the Cold War and quite apart from it), and a new one trying to be born. Old systems and worldviews were breaking down under the pressure of global economic, technological, environmental, and other forces; and new systems and worldviews capable of justly and peacefully managing the new economic, political, technological, and environmental problems we face had not yet been developed.

There was a tremendous lag in human development—a lag that was both spiritual and systemic. Systems of the heart and mind, and systems of more humane governance, needed to be developed to cope with the depth and scale of these changes.

We believed that those of us living in these times were being challenged to new levels of creativity and cooperation to forge a path through the present confusion and uncertainties toward a more viable and humane future for present and future generations. We were challenged to become the creative minority of which Toynbee had written—the creative minority who would, from deep spiritual commitment and motivation contribute to the development of a new civilization.

CHARACTERISTICS OF MAJOR TRANSFORMATIONS IN HISTORY

Historians suggest that in the whole span of human existence, humankind has previously experienced only two or three transformations comparable to the one we are now undergoing. These were:

1) The biological evolution from primate to hominid (pre-human) to homo sapiens, and the emergence of hunting and gathering societies and the Tribal Age over the last five million years. Within this longest period of human history came some of the greatest human developments, including the emergence of human consciousness, human speech, and tool making, symbol making, artistic, rational, and teaching/learning skills. Humans learned to live in community and developed social, political, economic, and educational systems appropriate for life in small kinship or familial tribal structures, and ethical, spiritual, or religious systems that emanated from their sense of powerful, sacred forces operative in Earth's processes. This

period encompasses 99 percent of human history.

2) The agricultural revolution and rise of The Age of Traditional Civilizations over the last 10,000 years. The agricultural revolution made possible a planned and surplus food supply and thus permanent settlements and cities. It also made possible role differentiation and specialization within societies, contributing to new developments in trade and economics, the arts, religion, education, and socio-political structures. This period gave birth to the rise of the great civilizations and world religions. Systems of governance shifted gradually from tribal structures to kingdoms and city-states and new ethical and normative systems appropriate for life in these traditional civilizations. In this period, too, the war system, class system, slavery, and patriarchy arose as full-fledged systems.

3) The scientific, industrial, humanistic revolutions that marked the breakdown of feudal structures and traditional civilizations and the rise of the Modern Age and Age of Nation States over the last 500 years. The modern scientific revolution, which began in Europe and was then exported around the world, made possible unprecedented gains in human longevity, health and wealth for those who benefited from it. It also had profound effects on worldviews and images of the Earth. Copernicus, Galileo, and Newton changed people's paradigm; the Earth was round, not flat, and not the center of the universe. Images of the primacy of God, gods, or a sense of the sacred were displaced and replaced by faith in man (masculine), machines, and nationalism—and later communism and other isms—to redeem and liberate humanity and produce happiness. The Earth was no longer sacred, but a place to be conquered and mastered by humans, and there transpired unprecedented human assaults and exploitation of the Earth. The war system was taken to new heights, with new

military technologies threatening the destruction of all life on Earth.

All these past transformations were notable for the following characteristics:

1) Crisis of growth. The Chinese use two characters to convey the concept of crisis. *Wei* means danger; breakdown; *chi* means new opportunity, breakthrough. In any crisis both possibilities exist. In periods of transition, social upheaval and crises occur as old structures and systems and worldviews break down and new worldviews and systems begin to emerge. Such crises can be characterized as crises of growth.

2) Rate of change. Each of the past transformations occurred more rapidly than previous ones. The present crisis of transition is especially acute. Past transformations occurred over centuries, and people had centuries to develop new worldviews, identity systems, and patterns of relationship. In contrast, we must make the transition to a global community in only a few decades.

3) Universality of change. Each past transformation occurred in different regions of the world at different times, sometimes thousands of years apart, but ultimately affected peoples in all world regions. The present transformation is global and is affecting all peoples in relatively the same time period.

4) Increasing interdependence. Each of these past transformations emerged out of widening circles of economic, environmental, social and political interdependence. Each involved new formulations of systems of identity, community, and loyalty.

5) Governance and political units. From clans and tribes, to city-states and kingdoms, to nation-states, each of these

transformations included changes in political structures, with the development of a public sector or polity at increasingly larger levels to manage the problems and opportunities resulting from increasing interdependence. The larger units did not necessarily eliminate smaller, local polities; more often they added a new layer to manage problems that could not be dealt with at the older, smaller levels. With new global scale interdependencies, and the problems of rapid globalization, effective global structures are needed to deal with problems that cannot be resolved locally or nationally. If global systems of governance are to be humane, and not destructive, they must be continually informed by values and norms that uphold human dignity, justice, peace, and ecological integrity.

6) New worldviews and relationships to the Earth. Each of these transformations also brought changes in the way human beings perceived the world and their relationship to the Earth.

7) Spirituality and images of the sacred. Each also brought changes in images of the sacred, and new forms of spirituality.

Most historians agree that we are now in the midst of another major transformation, one that is occurring more rapidly than any previous one and is global in scale. Some believe it will have more deep-reaching effects than any historical change since the emergence of human consciousness.

New communications, travel, and other technologies that advanced over the last several decades are weaving a web in which previously isolated and sovereign nation-states, and even formerly remote tribal societies, are now interconnected in economic, military, environmental, agricultural, technological, communications, and other interdependencies. All borders have become transparent and penetrable, and local and national self-interest is increasingly inseparable from global interest. The notion of national sovereignty is increasingly a fiction.

Decisions made in one part of the world—whether over the price of oil, interest or currency-exchange rates, bank scandals and failures, trade barriers, or greenhouse gases that cause global warming—affect every other country, and missiles aimed from thousands of miles away can penetrate all national borders. Music, movies, dance, sports, and other expressions of popular culture are shared across national lines. Professional development in virtually every field now involves or is affected by international communications. While some may seek to escape or retreat from the facts of increasing global interdependence, it is no longer practical to isolate ourselves within national boundaries.

The processes of globalization are accompanied by unprecedented problems that can no longer be resolved by employing old worldviews and/or only local or national systems of governance. Global forces are beyond the effective competence of individual nation-states. But the development of the necessary global vision, norms, policies, and structures to manage the problems and opportunities of a global age has not kept pace with these forces.

THREE WAYS OF LOOKING AT THE CURRENT TRANSFORMATION

In Gerald's and my work through GEA therefore, and in the challenge I am presenting in this article, the question is not whether we live in a time of breakdown and transformation, but rather how deep the breakdown goes, and what kind of breakthroughs we should expect or strive to attain. While many historians agree that we live in a time of major transformation, there is disagreement and uncertainty among them about the depth of the changes underway, and what values, worldviews, and social, economic, and political systems are likely to emerge in the new, global period we are entering. There are at least three levels or timeframes of analyses. None is exclusive of the others, but each carries its own set of implications and challenges for the future, including whether to expect the emergence of a global civilization and what, if any, forms of global governance are likely to emerge.

Fifty Year Time Frame

The first view sees the current moment as the breakdown of a fifty-year time period. What is breaking down is the world order shaped by the victors of World War II. The international institutions created in 1944 and 1945 to deal with the monetary, trade, economic, and security problems of a post-war world are now inadequate in the face of new global economic, environmental, and political realities of the 21st century. The two-thirds of the world that had no voice in establishing these institutions are now pushing for democratization of, or a greater voice in, the UN Security Council, International Monetary Fund, World Bank, World Trade Organization, and other multilateral structures.   Japan and Germany, crushed militarily and economically after the war, are now among the richest and most economically powerful countries. They seek positions in multi-lateral institutions commensurate with their new position and related international responsibilities.   The United Nations, which had been given a mandate to deal with threats to international peace and security (but was given insufficient power to deal effectively even with this mandate), is now faced by a new set of expectations for which it has no clear mandate or mechanisms: to deal with intra-national threats to peace and security—e.g., inter-ethnic or inter-religious strife contained within national borders and presumably under national prerogatives.

This view also includes the breakdown of the bipolar system created in the Cold War that followed World War II. In this bipolar system the rest of the world was dominated by two superpowers—the US and USSR—and their allies, who maintained a perverse form of peace through the threat of mutually assured destruction. Under this bipolar system, the United Nations could play only a marginal role in the maintenance of peace and security—certainly much less than most of the world had hoped. For almost five decades, the United Nations Security Council was often blocked by the veto of one or the other major power. Moreover, the United Nations was not equipped to deal with the nuclear threat, which could always be used to trump UN peace initiatives.

When the UN Charter was drafted in 1945, none of the delegates from the 51 founding nations knew anything about top secret efforts in the US to build atomic weapons. And so the UN was brought into existence without effective means to manage this new threat. In the resulting vacuum, the maintenance of international peace and security was primarily a prerogative of the superpowers under balance-of-power arrangements. With the end of the Cold War, this bipolar system broke down, and in its place a unipolar system is emerging, dominated by the US and its military allies in NATO. The peace dividends expected at the end of the Cold War have not been realized. Instead, militarism and rule by threat continues in both old and new forms. Nuclear weapons continue to be stockpiled and the global arms trade is a thriving business. Ethnic conflicts and genocide formerly contained by superpower coercion have vented their ugly heads, leaving millions of bodies strewn across the killing fields of parts of Africa, the former Yugoslavia, and elsewhere.

For awhile it had seemed that a trend toward regional security approaches would blossom into a new world order in which each world region maintained peace among its member states. Region by region the use of force would be replaced by the force of reason. But these regional arrangements, where they exist, are still too weak to assure world peace and security for the future. Even in Europe, where regional structures are stronger than elsewhere, the weak and under-funded Organization for Security and Cooperation in Europe (OSCE) was supplanted by NATO and the use of military force to resolve the crisis in former Yugoslavia. Although NATO is also a regional organization, the fact that it was a military branch of one of the sides in the Cold War, suggests that (a) the Cold War is not fully over, or if over, is not yet dead and buried and could rise again; and/or (b) the unipolar vision of world order currently carries more currency than more benign or less violent visions of regional security.

This fifty year view assumes that further shifts in world order will occur within the framework of the nation-state system and that the order that eventually emerges will remain essentially state-centric, with national governments being the main actors, and national sovereignty upheld as a core principle around which peace, security, and the well-being of peoples is assured. Within that frame a de facto form of global governance may evolve through default or design; this could be a continuation of a unipolar system, with the rest of the world continuing to be dominated by, and entrusting peace and security to, the remaining superpower, or it could be a further entrenchment and elaboration of a multi-polar international system, such as de facto rule by the Group of Seven, in which a consortium of a few economically rich and powerful nations make decisions that govern the rest, with little or no input from them—amounting to global governance by an international oligarchy. Or it could follow Huntington's scenario of a new world order that is both multi-polar and multi-civilizational, with a new balance of power emerging along cultural divisions.

A third alternative within the framework of the existing nation-state system has more democratic features. It involves (a) democratizing and strengthening the United Nations system to give the "two-thirds world" who were subordinated during the Cold War an equal say in decisions affecting them; and/or (b) promoting and further developing regional arrangements for peace and security. In these alternatives global governance is not left to chance, but is approached as a matter of responsible choice and participation.

Five Hundred Year Time Frame

A second view agrees with some of the above, but goes deeper. It sees the current transformation as the breakdown of a 500-year period characterized by the rise of the nation-state system, Enlightenment and secular-humanist ideals, Euro-American colonial and neo-colonial domination, and the spread of capitalism culminating in its near globalization.

Within this framework, some see shifts occurring within the existing nation-state system, including a redistribution of power and wealth away from Euro-American control and toward other states, such as the industrialized countries of Asia which have become powerful competitors in the global market place; others see a shift away from the nation-state system itself. The origin of the state-centric system around which the present world order is constituted is usually given as the 1648 Peace of Westphalia; this treaty ended both the Eighty Years War between Spain and the United Provinces of the Netherlands, and the Thirty Years' War (really a fifty-year struggle) in which the Austrian Hapsburgs and German princes battled for the European balance of power. The treaty gave full sovereignty to the member states of the Holy Roman Empire and launched the modern nation-state system, sometimes called the Westphalian system.

Although many people now take the nation-state system for granted and assume it is the final form in political evolution, when viewed within the long sweep of history it still seems very new, and its lasting capacity is unproven. Only in the 20th century did it become a near universal system as peoples from tribal societies, traditional civilizations, and former colonies were brought within its embrace. More than 100 new nation-states came into existence in the twentieth century, most of them in the second half.

The United Nations has wrongly been seen by some as a form of world government, or as a new form of world order superceding the state system. But the UN is not itself a state or government; it is an organization of states, governed by and for states, with a mandate to uphold the principle of state sovereignty. The UN cannot tell member states what to do; on the contrary, the member states are the masters who tell the UN what to do and they control its budget. In short, the UN is, in essence, an extension of the state-centric system.

So future historians may well look back and name the twentieth century the Century of Nation-States. But on a closer look, they could just as well name it the Century that began the Breakdown of the Nation State System and the Rise of Global Systems. For, despite the apparent success and near universality of the state-centric system by the end of the 20th century, it had no sooner reached its zenith than its core principle—state sovereignty—began to be eroded by the forces of globalization.

This is not to say that the nation-state will soon go out of existence; as a form of political organization it has proven very resilient. However, it suffers from a certain "Goldilocks syndrome"; while it is just right for addressing some problems, it is too large for resolving local problems, and too small for resolving problems that are global. While the nation-state will remain an important unit of political organization and decision-making for national level problems, it is an inadequate level of organization for dealing with global market forces and economic and ecological interdependencies, or for assuring peace and security in the 21st century. The power of the nation-state is also being eroded by the emergence of other actors and new power arrangements at global and regional levels, ranging from transnational corporations, cartels, and regional economic and trade regimes, to regional systems of governance such as the European Parliament.

The flow of economic power away from the nation-state is palpable. Of the world's hundred largest economies only 49 accrue to nation-states; the majority—51—are internal to corporations. Two hundred corporations, with interlocking boards and strategic alliances, now control 29 percent of world economic activity.[11] And while some corporations now have more wealth and power than most nation-states, they are not subject to the same democratic accountability that binds most national governments, and can function outside the effective control of national laws simply by moving to another country. A de facto new world order is already forming beyond the parameters of the nation-state system or democratic controls. There is as yet no effective form of global governance to assure that their behavior does not harm the global common good.

If aggregate economic growth is one's only—or primary—criterion of human well being, this trend may not be a cause of

---

[11] United Nations Conference on Trade and Development, World Investment Report 1996. as quoted in Hunger in a Global Economy, *Bread for the World*, 1998 Report on Hunger.

alarm for some people. In the 20th century the global economy grew seventeen-fold, from an annual output of $2.3 trillion in 1900 to $39 trillion in 1998. The growth in economic output in just three years—from 1995-1998—exceeded that during the 10,000 years from the beginning of agriculture up to the year 1900.[12] Per capita income multiplied four times, from $1,500 to $6,600, with most of this increase coming in the second half of the century. Life expectancy increased from 35 years in 1900 to 66 in 1999. More food was produced in the 20th century than ever before, and human products poured into an increasingly global marketplace at a record rate. Coupled with economic growth, advancements in science, medicine, industry, and technology made it possible for more people than ever before to live longer, healthier, and more productive lives.

From an aggregate view these trends seem to spell tremendous human success. But the benefits of this growth were not evenly distributed. While one fifth of the world population now live better lives than ever before, another one fifth struggle to survive with no or little access to safe water, or adequate nutrition, shelter, education, or employment. The stark contrasts are laid before us in a *Bread for the World Report*:

Consider this: If trade were evenly spread around the land surface of the world, the inhabitants of each square mile, including Antarctic penguins and Saharan camels, would have more than $62,000 in products to trade each year. But it is not. The thousands of women who sew sneakers in Indonesia together make less than Michael Jordan gets for endorsing them. □

---

[12] *Ibid*, p. 10.

This gap is compounded by the foreign debt of many of the poorest countries. Rich and poor countries alike are confronted by the need to survive growing global competition for favorable balances of trade and payments, and for access to scarce resources, markets, and new technologies. But the poorest countries that have borrowed heavily from international banks and agencies struggle under burdens of debilitating foreign debts, rising interest rates, adverse terms of trade, interrupted financial flows, and conditions imposed by lending agencies. Poor countries' debts cause not only hunger, disease and illiteracy among people at home; the violent conflict and refugee flows incited by these conditions reach beyond borders to affect people in creditor countries as well.

The power of the nation-state is being challenged from below as well as above. Even while governance is increasingly being ceded to global market forces, many national governments struggle with equally volatile domestic forces. A wave of inter-ethnic, inter-religious, and separatist conflicts have beset some countries, weakening -- in some cases even obliterating -- national government and the state. The lack of a constituted state or national governments has left some African populations in a perilous state, at the mercy of warlords, terrorists or economic collapse.

The United Nations, as a state-centric system required to uphold the principle of state sovereignty, has neither the mandate nor means to respond quickly and effectively to protect the sovereignty of peoples within countries fractured by internal warfare, gross violations of human rights, or ethnic cleansings and genocides. The question of humanitarian intervention, although much discussed, still does not have clear criteria or mechanisms for superceding national sovereignty. The UN has also come up against the limits of state sovereignty in its efforts to deal with such international problems as disarmament and arms control, terrorism, trafficking in drugs, women, and children, the spread of HIV-AIDS and other diseases, environmental degradation, and other global concerns that cannot be resolved within the framework of unlimited state sovereignty. As we go further into an increasingly global age, the UN will either continue to erode along with the state-system that created it, or it must be greatly reformed and strengthened to meet both intranational and trans-national challenges in the 21st century.

The need for a global polity or global structures of governance to deal with global problems becomes more and more manifest every day. On a positive note, the twentieth century saw a series of efforts to develop international structures and polities for international peace and security. A first attempt was made at the end of the 19th and beginning of the 20th centuries with two international peace meetings at the Hague aimed at arms control and disarmament and the development of a concert of nations. These negotiations were too slow to prevent World War I. A second attempt at an international polity was made after the war, producing the League of Nations. But, reluctant to surrender any sovereignty to the new international body, the founding states left it too weak to stop Hitler and prevent World War II.

A third attempt at a global order, initiated by the allied forces before the end of World War II, resulted in the United Nations. The UN became a midwife to the historic process of de-colonization and the entry into the international organization of many newly independent states. And through its specialized agencies it fostered international cooperation around a wide variety of issues, including economic development, education, environmental protection, food sufficiency, health care, housing, human rights, population, the advancement of women, and many other issues. The UN specialized agencies now constitute an important global infrastructure for global cooperation and policy development; however, once more the founding states were reluctant to delegate sufficient sovereignty, leaving the UN system too weak to deal effectively with many of the military, economic, ecological, and other transboundary crises that now beset the world.

However, the UN system does not represent a final form of polity for dealing with transnational issues; it is an evolving structure. Over its first five decades the UN showed that it was a living organism with a capacity to learn, adapt, and respond to new problems within the limits and constraints imposed by its member states. Future historians may one day consider the UN we have now to have been an embryonic form of a global polity, or a stepping stone to it. With political will the UN could be strengthened and developed into an effective global organization to serve the needs of people and the planet in the interdependent world of the 21st century.

Parallel with the development of inter-governmental organizations (IGOs), such as those that are part of the UN system, has been the development of thousands of international non-governmental organizations (INGOs) and civil-society organizations. The first INGOs began emerging as early as the 4th century and were primarily religious communities with international membership. From the 4th to the 19th centuries the number of INGOs grew relatively slowly: the *Yearbook of International Organizations* needed only three pages to list all of those that existed in some 1500 years. But in the 20th century their numbers skyrocketed. In contrast to 176 international non-governmental organizations in 1909, by 1985 there were 18,000. These INGOs have international memberships and function across national borders in the pursuit of common goals ranging from athletic, artistic, educational, professional, scientific, and religious, to issue concerns such as human rights, development, environmental protection, and peace. They constitute an emerging global civic infrastructure that functions outside the traditional nation-state system. Today, thousands of non-governmental and civil society groups have representatives observing at the United Nations who are trying to influence global-level policy development. Where once states were the only legitimate actors in international affairs, now citizen groups and other sectors are claiming the right to a place at the global policy table. Local authorities, labor and trade unions, professional associations, business and industry, religious networks, and civil society groups are all beginning to see themselves as global citizens – responsible members of a global as well as a local and national community.

In some cases local authorities and civil society groups are doing more to implement global agreements than the national governments who negotiated them. An example is Agenda 21, the international plan of action for environment and development agreed to at the 1992 Earth Summit in Rio de Janeiro. While most national governments have lagged behind in implementing this international agreement, some 18,000 local communities around the world have adopted their own local versions of Agenda 21. These communities are no longer content to wait for national governments to do something about the destruction of the environment. Nor do they believe it is enough to petition governments to act. Rather, with a new maturity, citizen groups are getting together among themselves, and negotiating, developing, and promoting new policies to deal with global-scale problems beyond the competency of any one of their states. In many ways these citizen groups are freer than national leaders to work across national lines in search of solutions to shared global problems.

In this view of transformation, then, the nation-state will continue to exist and play an important -- but not the only -- role in international and global affairs.   New forms of governance will emerge at the global level. And new forms of global polity will bubble up from below.

However, it is not yet clear what these forms will be.   We could continue to drift, as we are now, toward an order in which global governance continues to be ceded to market forces and where more and more wealth and power flow into fewer and fewer hands; or we could decide to develop more democratic, participatory forms of global governance -- either a greatly reformed UN or a new global organization that includes a stronger role for civil society.   This would require reconceptualizing sovereignty as something residing less in the state and more in the people; it would also require that nation-states pool and delegate some of their sovereignty in a restructured UN or new global organization, to make it effective in addressing issues beyond the competence of single nation-states.

Ten Thousand Year Time Frame

A third view agrees with the above analyses, but goes still deeper.   It sees the breakdown of a ten thousand year time frame dating from the agricultural revolution and the rise of traditional civilizations and the great world religions.   In this period, the myth of dominance took root and grew in the human imagination and in some belief structures.   This myth was given expression in the war system and related systems of class and caste, slavery, racism, ageism, and patriarchy, and various other forms of hierarchical structure that pitted one human group over and against another. Together these systems of dominance comprised a total system governing human development and the direction of human history.   Everything was affected—political, social, economic, cultural, and religious structures and relationships. The myth of dominance extended not only to inter-human relations, but also to human-Earth relations, in that some human groups began to see themselves as separate from, and over, the Earth, leading in the modern period to unprecedented human assaults on the natural world.

In this third view, what is now breaking down is the whole myth structure underlying systems of human dominance. These worldviews and systems are becoming dysfunctional to human survival and unacceptable to growing numbers of people in an increasingly interdependent world.

For evidence, those who espouse this view point to the growing waves of people struggling for democracy and liberation around the world over the last several hundred years, from the Enlightenment philosophers and the American and French revolutions in the 18th century, to movements for the abolition of slavery and for women's suffrage beginning in the 19th century, to the 20th century movements for racial justice, civil rights, women's rights, and an end to apartheid. They also point to anti-colonial and independence movements, and human rights and peace movements, all pushing for greater realization of human dignity and participation; and to the environmental movements that in the latter part of the 20th century began to appear everywhere around the world, challenging people to reassess their relationships with the Earth and to learn to re-inhabit the Earth as responsible and functioning members of the larger community of life.

As the myth of dominance continues to be challenged, what is emerging in its place is a new vision of our common dependency on one Earth and our mutual interdependence with one another.   The emphasis is on solidarity, mutuality, participation, and community; on horizontal rather than hierarchical relationships; and on the health and wholeness of persons and planet.

The old paradigm of dominance was given credence not only in some religious teachings, but also modern scientific views that were atomistic and hierarchical. The Earth was depicted as a great machine with separately acting parts; humans were seen as the apex and masters of its life. Now a new paradigm is emerging from science; actually, it is not entirely new, for our tribal ancestors and spiritual visionaries through the ages have intuitively understood what scientists are now proving empirically: that the Earth is like a single cell in the universe, and humans are not over the cell, but part of it. We will live or die as this single cell lives or dies. The question of human survival and security is inseparable from the functioning integrity of the larger Earth community.

The spiritual, psychological, religious, political, economic, and environmental implications of this view are profound. The transformation envisioned is not a mere matter of tinkering with political policies or passing new laws. It involves turning upside down the way we think, and accepting a new, more mature and responsible role in the further evolution of the planet. It means taking responsibility for the state of our souls and for the state of the world.

For we have new powers never dreamed of by our ancestors; powers to destroy or to build the Earth. In the 20th century we stockpiled weapons around the Earth beyond anything imagined in previous centuries. We buried millions of mines in the Earth, which now kill and maim the world's children. We produced thousands of nuclear, chemical, and biological weapons and threatened one another with mutually assured destruction. The weapons created in the name of defending ourselves were so destructive they could not be used without killing those they were supposed to protect as well as those against whom they were aimed. Whatever purpose the war system might once have served, it has now become dysfunctional to future human survival, yet it has not been abolished.

In the 20th century we also learned how to intervene in the DNA, the delicate genetic coding that evolved through eons of natural selection, and how to create new species in test tubes and clone old ones, with as yet unforeseen consequences. We caused hundreds of thousands of plant and animal species to go out of existence by over-industrialization, deforestation, and toxic and radioactive pollution; a part of creation, a part of the divine, is lost forever. We are, through our human choices and actions, altering the face of the Earth, changing its climate, depleting its ozone layer, and rendering the planet uninhabitable for future generations. We are shaping the next stages of planetary evolution.

No other generation has had such powers over life and death—powers that in the past some only ascribed to God. Yet we have not developed the moral maturity and wisdom to use these new powers in ways that will assure a healthy future for our planet, our children, or ourselves. There has been a tragic lag in our development. These new powers demand that we now overcome this spiritual and ethical lag; that we become more morally mature and wiser human beings than any previous generation. We must become spiritually attuned and conscious co-participants with the sacred processes at work on the planet, in the cosmos, and in ourselves.

In this view, we are moving toward a planetary civilization requiring new myths, a far deeper, more globally inclusive spirituality and ethic, and new understandings and relationships to one another and the Earth. A successful transition would be characterized by a greater sense of wholeness, interconnectedness, and mutuality in inter-human and human-Earth relations. It would be a shift away from competitive and toward more cooperative social models; away from the excessive individualism of Western capitalism and the excessive communalism of communism and toward a stronger embrace of unity and diversity within concentric circles of community at local, regional, and now global levels; away from "my nation (or racial or ethnic group) above all others" and toward an embrace of cultural and religious pluralism with mutual rights and responsibilities for all peoples; away from oppressor/oppressed and win/lose models and toward win/win and partnership models in mutual service to the larger human and Earth communities.

Is such a vision of transformation realistic? Those holding this view do not consider themselves dreamers; they point to many positive signs of such a transformation already underway. To the evidence already mentioned above they add the growing interest of people in a new cosmology and Earth-based spirituality; organic and community-based agriculture and holistic health movements that have worked their way from the fringes into mainstream journals, institutions and businesses; and the engagement of scientists, community organizers, political leaders, and people from virtually every profession and religion in care of the Earth. They point also to growing movements to ban the proliferation and trade in weapons, from hand guns and assault rifles to land mines and nuclear weapons. They point to gains in human rights in the 20th century, including the Universal Declaration of Human Rights and the whole body of international human rights law that followed, defining the obligations of states toward citizens. They point to gains made in rights for women around the world, including numerous international agreements and changes in the constitutions and laws of many countries against discrimination on the basis of gender. They also point to more than 150 international agreements for the protection of the environment, most of them in the latter part of the 20th century; although still weak in implementation, many of these new international agreements show an increasing consciousness of the need for international standards and norms and are laying the normative foundations for more responsible life in a global community.

Those holding this third view also point to the unprecedented level of cooperation across national lines in virtually every human pursuit—never before in history has there been so much global cooperation, and never before has there been such a vibrant global civil society working across national lines for our common global future.

But nothing is automatic. For this shift to succeed this generation must still overcome a tremendous learning lag. We must learn more in the next few decades than our ancestors had to learn in the last 10,000 years. We have to rethink what it means to be human, and how to re-inhabit the Earth and to live in community in new ways. We need to learn to live more intentionally, more consciously, and question our decisions hourly and daily, taking responsibility for their impact on the present and future life of the Earth and the human community. We need to learn to think in multi-generational terms, about the ways in which our decisions today will affect those yet to come—one, two, three, four, five, six, and seven generations into the future—because our choices made today have such profound consequences on the world of tomorrow.

AN AXIAL PERIOD OF HISTORY

If any of the above analyses are correct, the period of history ahead of us will evolve in ways significantly different from that of the 20th century. This is not merely the residue of millennial thinking. The above changes were underway well before the turn of the millennium, and they will continue evolving in one way or another in the 21st century and new millennium.

We live in an axial period of history, with major changes underway in political, economic, and social systems, and possibly also psycho-spiritual systems and structures of thought. Despite differences in the above analyses, they all assume that we are entering an age where local and national realities are increasingly penetrated by global forces, and that some reordering of structures at the global level is inevitable and essential. The question before us, then, is not whether a new world order will emerge in response to new global imperatives, but rather what kind of world order? Based on what worldview? What values? What ethic and ethos? What kind of leadership will guide and shape it? What kind of structures and systems will evolve to govern it? Who will benefit, and who will pay? Will it be a world order that oppresses and represses some for the sake of the many, or many for the sake of the few? One in which two thirds of the people remain poor, hungry, fearful, or a more equitable, humane, and less violent world order for all peoples? One that opens the way to truer freedom, with shared responsibility for the common good in a global community? Will it be a future where the life of the Earth is degraded, squandered, sold in the marketplace, and lost to future generations—or will it be built on new understandings of the integral relatedness we and our great-grandchildren have with our living Earth?

We do not know the answers with certainty. A new world order does not necessarily mean a better one. Converging and colliding trends portend that unless we change our direction, the world order that emerges in the 21st century could be a very nasty one, especially for those who are on the underside of existing systems of dominance.

A new world order may emerge in one of three ways: crisis, drift, or conscious, democratic choice of a preferred alternative. Each path is likely to generate a different outcome.

If a new world order comes through crisis—or multiple, inter-active crises such as the collapse of global economic, financial, communication, or ecological systems—the outcome is not likely to be more humane or democratic. A collapse of the international banking system, for example, could cause global panic leading to severe measures to restrain disorder. Major ecological changes, such as global climate change, loss of bio-diversity, or continuing loss of clean water and other vital resources, could intensify global competition for remaining resources, leading to wars over resources or to major civil unrest.   In the potentially chaotic climate of fear and uncertainty generated by the collapse of major systems, a despotic form of global governance, backed by military power, may be imposed on the world's peoples to prevent global anarchy.

The path of drift is not any more promising. If we continue as we are now to cede questions of global governance to the market system, we will beget an undemocratic world order, one in which increasing wealth flows into fewer and fewer corporate hands and critical decision-making is not the prerogative of citizens or their elected representatives, but of corporate boards and stockholders. Burying our heads in the sand and abdicating our responsibility for the outcome, or merely railing against the forces of economic globalization, will not change this undemocratic drift.

Positive alternatives need to be consciously envisioned and sought. Informed citizens in all cultures and world regions need to dialogue, negotiate, and work together to shape a more humane, participatory, and environmentally responsible world order. In contrast to the top-down models of world order that are likely to result from the crisis or drift scenarios, this third path would build a new world order from the bottom up, with the participation of strong, vibrant, and informed global citizens. If global governance in some form is inevitable and essential to coordinate decisions affecting our shared future in an interdependent world, then should it not be a form of global governance that is of the people, by the people and for the people and planet?

This we know: the vision and path that will ultimately prevail, and the form of global governance that ultimately evolves, will depend greatly on who is willing to participate now in shaping global systems, and on the worldviews and values they bring to the process. Those who do not participate also affect the outcome, by abdicating their choices to others.

This we know, too: the inner and outer dimensions of a new world order must advance simultaneously. If a future global civilization is to be more humane, we must expand our hearts, minds, souls, and consciousness as well as our political, economic, and social structures. The systems we develop must be able to assure present and future generations greater peace, economic well-being, ecological integrity, and human dignity than were realized on the blood-soaked killing fields of the 20th century. This is no small challenge.

A DEFINING MOMENT

This is, therefore, a defining moment and a deciding moment in the life of world. The vision and understandings we have and don't have, the decisions we make and don't make, the values and ethical standards we set and do not set, the actions we take and don't take now will make a major difference in shaping the world order of the 21st century.

This is also a time of uncertainty. Like Dr. Doolittle's two-headed Pushme-Pullyou, we are moving in seemingly opposite directions at the same time. Centrifugal forces that impel us toward global integration activate countervailing centripetal forces that seek more familiar identity systems at family, ethnic, or local community levels. With this tension pulling at the seams of our political, economic, cultural and psycho-spiritual systems, we must rise to new levels of creativity and cooperation. For better or worse, we now live in one global neighborhood with interlocked destinies. All our separate past histories are now converging toward one shared future history. Decisions and activities in one part of the world affect everyone else in the neighborhood. Our common security, peace, and mutual well-being require that we work together to shape norms, standards and systems that work for the benefit not only of some of us, but all of us.

RELIGIONS MATTER

In this defining moment, religions matter. Religion and spirituality have mattered for millions of years in helping to shape and maintain past civilizations, and they will matter in shaping a future global civilization.

History shows that the true shapers of past cultures and

civilizations have not been political leaders so much as spiritual leaders: Lao-tse, Confucius, Buddha, Abraham, Moses, Jesus, Paul, Mohammed, Baha'u'llah. Their teachings have shaped values and ethics, informed social systems, legitimized and de-legitimized political regimes, and evaluated the justice and injustice of economic systems. In short, religions have provided norms of behavior that, while not constituting government, constitute a powerful moral force—a governing force, a form of governance—in human affairs.

We also know that the role of religion (or more correctly, of people professing to act in the name of religion) has not always been positive. Religions have sometimes been powerful rivers that divide and separate us from one another. At times these dividing rivers have seemed impossible to cross in order to reach each other, hear and see each other, be with each other, and stand inside each others stories and histories. People professing religion have sometimes closed their eyes and ears to the hungry, the homeless, the imprisoned who were not of their ways and beliefs; they have sometimes been the cause of hunger and homelessness, and have themselves been the jailers and executioners. Organized religion has sometimes been a tool of the state, used to manipulate people toward blind obedience to state power; at times it has been indistinguishable from the state, wielding political power for its own gain. Religion has sometimes been a factor in genocide and war, used to justify killing all those who are "others."

Yet, all this needs to be distinguished from the authentically spiritual, the truly religious, which, if pursued to its core, leads to an experience of oneness.

The psychiatrist Carl Jung suggested that there is an important difference between authentic religion and religious creed. Creedal religion or collective belief runs the risk of becoming oppressive when, like a totalitarian state, it is imposed on people as an absolute and the individual is submerged in the mass authority. This is the opposite of authentic religion, which in Jungian terms is a living, "incontrovertible experience of an intensely personal relationship between [humans] and an extramundane authority." The religious impulse—called by some the search for God, by others ultimate concern, by others an awareness of our relatedness to a Ground of All Being, and by still others the path of liberation or salvation—is not something that can be superimposed. It is, says Jung, "an instinctive attitude peculiar in [humans]" and will seek its own course. Nor can it be separated from the so-called secular aspects of our existence without resulting in feelings of alienation or incompleteness.

The Latin word *religiare*, from which the word religion in many Western languages is derived, means to unify, to bind together again. In Sanskrit, one of the original meanings of *dharma* (eternal religion) is the same: "to bind together as one the whole universe." Religion has also been defined as the experience of harmony, of the holy or whole or ultimate; the experience of the sacred, the unknowable. Religion has evolved out of a human sense of a reality greater than the self, greater than the sum total of quantifiable physical, economic, political, or social facts and phenomena. For some, religion is an effort to discover order (cosmos) in disorder (chaos).

Religion is also a means by which societies interpret life and develop and reinforce codes of morality and conduct in keeping with these interpretations and the requirements of community life. Religion also includes those beliefs and practices by means of which a group designates its deepest problems of meaning, suffering and injustice, and specifies its most fundamental ways of trying to reduce those problems.

Moreover, religion, through its sacred stories and scriptures, often carries the symbols and archetypes by which a people coalesce and define their identity as a community, culture, or civilization.

RELIGION AS SOURCE AND RESOURCE

No wonder Toynbee, Huntington, and some other historians and social analysts have persisted in claiming that religions will play a central role in shaping a future world order. All the above definitions and understandings of religion suggest that religion is of immense significance for questions of world order. The converse is also true—world order is not peripheral to the world's religious and spiritual traditions; it is at the deepest core of religious meaning, experience, and interest. The world's religious and spiritual traditions are a valuable source of wisdom for a world struggling to find direction in a time of global transformation.

In addition to the spiritual meanings and content religions bring as sources for world order thinking, the major world religions also have networks of organizations, educational and health-care institutions, alumni networks, research institutes, spiritual communities, social and civic-action groups and programs. People in these networks can and often do operate across national lines with greater ease than government officials, unbound by the constraints that tie the hands of government actors. People of religion have been major actors in work for a more peaceful, equitable, and ecologically sustainable world order. They have contributed important scholarship and professional expertise to help resolve some of the grave issues confronting humanity. Their members, programs, and institutions put them in touch with leaders and shapers of global policy. They can be important partners and co-creators in developing a more compassionate and just world order.

If Toynbee's analysis above is right, our spiritual journeys now will be vitally important to the development of an emerging global civilization. Spiritual growth and transformation are as important as, and possibly more important than, political changes in global systems, for these inner transformations of soul and mind prefigure, inform, inspire, and sustain the outer work. The inner and outer world order—spiritual growth and the development of more humane global systems—are inseparable parts of a holistic world order. They develop in conformity to one another and are mutually reinforcing. We need to draw from our deepest spiritual sources and resources in nurturing a more humane world order.

TRIPLE UNIVERSAL ETHICS FOR A NEW CIVILIZATION

Chung Ok Lee, Ph.D

Dr. Chung Ok Lee was born in Korea and received full ordination in Won Buddhism in 1981. She is a graduate of New York University and holds a Ph.D. in Religious Education. Rev. Lee is Representative of Won Buddhism to the United Nations and Co-President of World Conference on Religion and Peace/International. Dr. Lee has served as President of the Committee of Religious NGO's at the United Nations, Co-President of the Oslo Conference on Freedom of Religion, Co-President of the Chicago Parliament of World's Religions, and Founding Co-Chair of the Values Caucus at the United Nations. Dr. Lee is a spiritual teacher, peace activist and scholar.

All religions and spirituality are based on a Common Source, all human beings and all forms of life are interdependent as One Earth Family, and all social, economic, religious and political enterprises have a Common Purpose.

Chung-san

The Triple Universal Ethics, 1961

INTRODUCTION

We are living in a new era marked with both positive and negative possibilities. The positive side of trends includes advancement of science and technology, democracies, the ideals of equality, freedom and justice, modern medicine, feminism and the universality of human rights. This positive side has changed human mentality from unreasonable to reasonable, isolation to interdependency and exclusiveness to inclusiveness. It has promoted democracy, transparency and participation of all.

The negative side of today's trends includes the harsh consequences of capitalism, materialism and consumerism. These trends have contributed to the globalization of problems including the environmental crisis and widespread poverty, the replacement of quality by quantity, and loss of meaning and values. This negative trend becomes the dominant culture in human society today resulting in human uncertainty, insecurity and dehumanization.

Both positive and negative trends have awakened human consciousness. Now is the time to search for new approaches and new solutions, not only for our own well being, but also for generations to come.

This article addresses issues regarding: 1) An Evolving New Civilization, 2) The Triple Universal Ethics: An Alternative Worldview, 3) The Common Source of the World's Religions, 4) One Earth Family: Ecological Paradigm, and 5) One Work Place: Global Interdependence.

AN EVOLVING NEW CIVILIZATION

As material civilization develops, cultivate spiritual civilization accordingly.

So-tae-san

The Scripture of Won Buddhism, 1916

A new civilization will be born from the global crisis such as overpopulation, environmental degradation, poverty, nuclear, chemical and biological threats.   The acceleration of these trends will generate an unavoidable need to undergo fundamental changes to survive as a human species on our planet.

No one will be exempt from this global crisis or the need to integrate profound modifications because the earth is truly the common denominator between all human beings and other species. If the planet is healthy then the earth serves as a vital life force. However, if the planet finds itself in crisis, death and destruction will ensue, and this development will contribute to unifying people to address this critical situation.

An over emphasis on the values of materialism and consumption and ignorance of our interconnected relationships with nature constitute some of the root causes of environmental degradation.   The effect of this environmental imbalance destroys the universal life force while reinforcing social inequalities and poverty. So-tae-san says:

> Due to the dominance of a scientific civilization, the human spirit grows weaker while materialism increasingly flourishes and asserts their domination over the enfeebled human spirit. Thus human beings find themselves chained

to the servitude of materialism.[1]

Materialism drives contemporary societies due to its power and prestige. The dominance of material values today impacts directly on the life of men and women and threatens the future of modern societies and the planet. When financial motivation takes hold of science and scientists, the humanitarian nature of the scientific spirit is seriously affected. Modern science exerts an enormous power over life and death.

Universality and Inclusiveness

Won Buddhism believes that humanity has "A Common Purpose as One Family living on One Planet Earth."[2] This new vision of Won Buddhism contributes to enhancing human solidarity and can lead to fundamental changes in human thoughts, attitudes and behaviors in every aspect of our lives. We must refocus our vision based upon interconnected relationships between human and nature. This integrated vision can be achieved through self-cultivation and enlightenment. It is capable of elevating humanity toward planetary consciousness and sustainability.

One of the major characteristics of a new civilization can be found in the values of universality and inclusiveness. There exists a deep connection between our own lives and the lives of others. Therefore, the building of a new civilization requires profound transformations in our relationship with other human beings and non-human beings.

A new civilization will nurture a balance between globalization and healthy localization to preserve a

---

[1] So-Tae-San, *The Scripture of Won Buddhism*, 1.
[2] *Ibid.*, 989.

multicultural world. Multicultural education will serve as the foundation for a new civilization and broaden our understanding of diverse local cultures. A universal message from diverse cultures could emerge and will enhance unity in diversity. It could also lead to a spiritual transformation that would transcend the confines of local cultures. It could reduce bias and prevent conflict. Multicultural understanding is an important approach in conflict resolution in the areas where cultural and religious clashes take place.

The new global civilization implies that all cultures respect each other. This new civilization further implies acceptance of each other, inclusiveness, and open mindedness, without the divide between "us and them." In order to achieve this, mind cultivation becomes a necessity. Thus in the words of Samuel Huntington:

> Meanings and sources of universal civilization at the present moment are based on Western political and economic domination over non-Western societies. The expansion of the West has promoted both the modernization and Westernization of non-Western society. [3]

In that sense true globalization should avoid the dominance of one culture over the other. International institutions must therefore, engage in partnership with civil society.

In new civilization is characterized by universality and inclusiveness that require true democratic system. Democracy is a system that represents individual empowerment, self-

---

[3] Huntington, Samuel. *The Clash of Civilizations: Remaking of World Order*. (Simon & Schuster: New York, 1997), 66.

cultivation and equality. We need to modify the composition of the power structure of democracy to become a reflection of the people it serves. This can be achieved by ensuring that all humans have equal access to the power structures as well as the process of leadership cultivation. By empowering the voices of the minority and powerless which have been neglected or silenced for too long, one could reap the benefits of cultivating the wisdom that stems from diversity.

Spiritual Civilization

The twentieth century was a century of science. The twenty-first century will be a spiritual century. Unless human beings are elevated to be spiritual enough to practice ethical and spiritual values at all levels, humanity may not survive the third millennium.

A new civilization will partly be developed through peoples' movements and the spiritual empowerment of individuals and groups. More people will increasingly participate and engage in shaping their own future. The information superhighway and democracy could be seen as two vehicles driving the people's movements to a level of a global significance.

Spiritual practice cultivates inner strength, confidence, inspiration, commitment and sense of purpose. We should address spiritual needs as well as material needs, spiritual poverty as well as material poverty. Only if the scientific civilization can be integrated with the inner spiritual civilization can mutual harmony and an ideal global society be established in the world. Spirituality may nurture moral, ethical and spiritual transformation, which are the keys unlocking the door to our interconnectedness and interdependence.

The contemporary world needs moral leadership. One of the guiding principles for multi-integration in this New World is: "As material civilization develops, cultivate spiritual civilization accordingly."[4] A political, economic, technological, and scientific revolution without a concomitant spiritual revolution is certain to lead us to a world of desolation, a garden without flowers, arid land without water anywhere. Furthermore, we must be prepared to meet the demands of an increasing spiritual thirst, as recently evidenced by religious resurgence in the former Soviet Union, in central and Eastern Europe and in Latin America as well as North America.

The process of creating the blueprint for systemic change must be based upon an examination of the root of our global problems.   Through an internal, individual, community, national and global dialogue a new vision of solutions and a corresponding action plan can be designed.   This blueprint must rework the framework and policies of existing economic, governmental, religious, educational, and media power structures.   The basis of this entire transformation must arise from fundamental changes in human values and spiritual belief systems that are now driven by dualism, materialism, ignorance, and arrogance.

Ironically even with the abundance of wealth, resources and technology on earth today human problems are still increasing. We urgently need to redirect wealth and technology. We need to dedicate ourselves to saving our planetary home by recognizing that human destiny and the earth are deeply interdependent.

In 1916, So-Tae-San, founder of Won Buddhism envisioned One Earth Community in a universal and cosmic

---

[4] *The Scripture of Won Buddhism*, 82.

interdependence will bring people of all continents, all races and all religions together to face a common future. This vision provides fundamental moral principles for peaceful coexistence of the world community, promoting peace and justice, expanding love and compassion to all. In order to actualize this new vision, humanity needs to integrate material and spiritual values. It requires a more mature humanity that practices self-examination and self-criticism of one's own tradition and institutions.

This civilization will be based upon an advanced state of intellectual, cultural, spiritual and material development in human society. Through a dynamic peoples' movement, this new vision and resulting civilization will emerge.

TRIPLE UNIVERSAL ETHICS: AN ALTERNATIVE WORLDVIEW

We are called, you and I, by the voice of the Good, and the voice of the True and the voice of the Beautiful, called exactly in those terms, to witness the liberation of all sentient beings without exception.[5]

Ken Wilber

The Marriage of Sense and Soul, 1998

In 1961, Chung-San, So-Tae-San's successor, proclaimed the Triple Universal Ethics. It was the first appeal to humanity to recognize the need for universal ethics in the world. The Triple Universal Ethics provides an alternative worldview:

---

[5] Ken Wilber, *The Marriage of Sense and Soul: Integrating Science and Religion*, (Random: New York, 1998), 214.

"Within One Source and with One Principle, as One Family within One Household, as Co-workers on One Work Place, we can build One Earth Community!"[6] This Triple Universal Ethics also contributes a philosophical framework describing a universal and even cosmic interdependent world.

With inner changes of consciousness and spiritual development paralleling the advancement of science and technology, humanity will realize that we share a Common Source, are interrelated as One Family and have a Common Purpose.   This is a revolutionary philosophy, which will deepen human consciousness and will lead to a new vision based on spiritual values. The crisis in modern civilization lies not in material poverty, but in spiritual poverty and the decline of ethical judgment and moral obligation.   Humanity is searching for a system of values appropriate for the new era, which will strengthen and redeem the human spirit. In order to do this, we need a new ethical framework that is radically different from traditional values. The Triple Universal Ethics offers a new worldview for the entire earth community and offers a new system of values appropriate for a new civilization.

Shared Values and Ethics

A new civilization should improve the quality of all forms of life based on shared values and ethics. We need to forge shared values on global responsibility and governance to solve problems facing humanity today.   It is inspiring to see a growing number of people dedicate themselves to searching for the new ideas and values necessary for human survival. We need to develop good governance based on universal ethics and values in order to build a more enlightened society. It requires

---

[6]*The Scripture of Won Buddhism*, 989-991.

nurturing unity in diversity, reverence, cooperation, freedom, compassion and solidarity. Shared values can be developed through cross-cultural, cross professional, cross-generational dialogues. Universal Ethics should include ways to integrate mind and body, the secular and the sacred, theory and practice, science and religion.

The Triple Universal Ethics are applicable in an interconnected world as a new principle, philosophy and ethic. This philosophy of Oneness requires an ethical commitment and continued practice to transform individuals, communities and institutions toward a new civilization. In order to change we need to understand our world, other forms of life and the meaning of spiritual Oneness. This worldview is radically different from the traditional dualistic worldviews.

In this philosophy of Oneness, ethnicities and nationalities are different, but humanity is considered One Family based on One Life Energy. Opinions and methods may differ but we have a Common Purpose to live in peace with justice. People come from different walks of life, but have a common goal that is to build a better world. All social, political economic and religious enterprises must utilize their vast and unique resources for the betterment of humanity.

Building a Paradise on Earth

The Triple Universal Ethics is a practical application of a religious vision and ideal society. A religious dream of paradise is a symbol of hope and human aspiration for a better life in the future. This religious dream is pointing to an ideal place, especially in its social, political, and moral aspects. This religious dream of an ideal society is related to the religious understanding of the end of time and the beginning of a new history. So-tae-san predicted that a more civilized moral world

is coming and moral obligation will prevail. Now is the end of
the Old World and the beginning of a New World. The end of
time means the end of darkness, domination, ignorance,
subjugation, suffering and discrimination. The beginning of a
new history means that it is time for the beginning of openness,
liberty, equality, independence, prosperity and a paradise on
earth. It is the time of a great opening of a new heaven and a
future, which leads to the triumph of goodness.[7]

A new civilization will attempt to build a paradise on earth
by integrating material and spiritual values. We expect that this
will be a long term process. Science and technology should be
directed to inspire a moral obligation towards the building of a
new civilization. Advancements of science and technology
demand ethical, spiritual, and religious leaders to influence the
direction of these advancements. Today technology challenges
unbreakable principles and traditionally non-changeable areas.
Science is developing the ability to alter the essence of life
itself by eliminating criminal tendencies and "purifying" the
human species through gene modification. This raises ethical
concerns that may unite ethical, scientific and religious leaders
to renew their obligation to work together, overriding religious
exclusiveness. Religion has been dedicated to purifying human
deeds such as hatred, desires, crime, violence, and greed.
Dialogue between religion and science will be crucial to deal
with our human future and the ethical use of technology to
ensure the benefits of these advancements are shared by all.

In the coming era, the global new civilization will utilize
all the potentials of human beings. Our global problems are
man-made problems. Therefore, we must awaken the human

---

[7]Chung Ok Lee. "Soteasan's Dream of America," *Human Civilization
and Won Buddhist Thought*, (Won Buddhism Press; Korea, 1991), 1870.

capacity to counterbalance and search for the solutions from a higher consciousness. We need to teach how to empower human beings spiritually in order to become creators and participants in building their future. Respecting the dignity of each human will increase everyone's awareness and responsibility to accept the consequences of their behaviors and choices.

THE COMMON SOURCE OF THE WORLD'S RELIGIONS

All religions and churches must understand their foundation of the common source. This understanding can bring a greater harmony among different religious traditions.

Chungsan

Triple Universal Ethics, 1961

One of major challenges of the 21st century is to build harmony among different religious traditions and sects. The heart of each culture is a religion, which offers an explanation of the ultimate meaning of life and ethics. As Huntington stresses, "In the modern world, religion is a central, perhaps *the* central force that motivates and mobilizes people."[8] Through globalization, national boundaries become less important and the role of government is getting weaker. However the power and influence of religion may be stronger than governments to mobilize people for either good or bad cause.

In the evolving new civilization, religion will no longer be a source of conflict. Religions will become part of the solution

---

[8] *The Clash of Civilizations*, 66.

and reconciliation process. Often the intolerance of political diversity, just as the overindulgence of political unity, manifests itself in hideous violence in the world. It is sad but important to remember that religion is not immune from this type of manifestation. Practically every remaining and persisting international conflict on the earth is caused, nourished or intensified by religious factors, differences, intolerance or fundamentalism.

In the past, religions had a tendency to ignore, dominate and absorb the other religions. This attitude has created serious religious conflicts and clashes of cultures. For thousands of years religious differences have often been a cause of animosity and even bloodshed in spite of fundamental teachings of love, peace, justice and hope.

Religious leaders need courage to confront the very real problems facing the human family and our troubled world. Dominant religions in each culture must initiate the building of new bridges of cooperation across old chasms of bitterness and misunderstanding with other religious traditions.

A most urgent step in building cooperation and mutual understanding is that religious leaders and clergy of every tradition must stop preaching divisive messages based upon superiority. One of the main causes of religious discrimination is the teaching of this divisive message by claiming that *my religion is the only religion and has the only truth.* The danger of the only religion or truth has created many holy wars. People are taught to be intolerant and cruel to others' religions.

We have to reexamine our thoughts, conscience and religions and see whether we subtly promote religious segregation, distinction, restriction or exclusiveness. Many intelligent people in the secular society are critical of the role of religion because of this divisive message that causes religious conflicts. Religious leaders must empty religious egoism, arrogance and be humble-minded.

Religion has a crucial role to play in building a new civilization because it is one of the most powerful institutions dealing with minds and hearts. Religious traditions are fountains of values. The world's religions advocate the ethical and spiritual qualities of love, hope, peace, justice and wisdom. Religion provides the vision for humanity and should act as a primary constructive force to create a peaceful, harmonious global village.

Religious wisdom can help to further the growth of humanity's ethical consciousness in an age of global interdependence. We need to initiate a creative dialogue between the leaders of spiritual and religious traditions on the causes, results, and solutions of the escalating world crisis. World religious leaders need to clarify values and doctrines that will help this new civilization evolve. If properly mobilized, they have great potential to exercise their power and reach millions of people even as quickly as over a weekend.

One Source and Many Paths

In their essence, many religions throughout the world share the same message and teach the same Truth. However their systems and teachings have been practiced in such different ways that misunderstandings have occurred. This is the result of ignoring the original principle from which each denomination and sect was derived.[9] Through the evolution of consciousness humanity has the capacity to recognize that the teachings of all sects, schools, and denominations of world religions are pointing to a Common Source. They can come to

---

[9] *The Scripture of Won Buddhism*, 2.

the same conclusions by returning to the founding vision of their particular religion.

We need a new universal ethic for the world religions to play a positive role in the world. The first of the Triple Universal Ethics calls for a fundamental change in our understanding of religion by pointing to their Common Source. It stresses that all great religions are from a Common Source even though they have different ways of practice. God, Tao, Dharmakaya, Ir-Won, Ultimate Reality, Self, Life Energy, The Creator, Supreme Being are different names of the Common Source.[10]

There are many paths to reach the top of the mountain. When we attain right enlightenment, we will realize that there are many different names for the Common Source.

The essence of world religions is like finger pointing to the moon, a symbol of the Common Source. There are many fingers pointing at the one true moon. All religious teachings and scriptures can be compared to finger pointing. The finger itself is not the moon. There are many fingers that are pointing to the moon but there is only one moon in the sky. Each religious tradition can be compared to finger pointing and the moon is the Common Source. Through fingers, we must see the real moon. Throughout history, world religions have promoted the same message and re-proclaimed it according to different times and cultures

Religion for Public Debate

Due to religion's capacity to be both positive and negative, religious traditions must learn how to understand themselves in

---

[10] *Ibid.*, 100.

the eyes of other religions and non-religious people. In this new era, world religions need to be ready to modify their perspectives and messages in order to engage modern society. Therefore, religious leaders must allow public debate on religion.[11] If religion is to become the central force to mobilize people, it is critical for religious leaders to be politically concerned, socially engaged, culturally sensitive and informed.

Since religion is a part of the problem, they must have a public debate. Religions need to be reformed in order to participate in the future of humanity. Public debate will assist religion to serve humanity more effectively.

These public debates will identify obstacles and hindrances. It is our task and our duty to curb and eventually eliminate violence from our earth. Essential to the accomplishment of this task is the cultivation of people's spiritual nature. Public debate will encourage people to eliminate the weeds of greed, egocentrism, and ambition that threaten to choke the life in our spiritual garden where peace and justice reign.

If we have public debate on religion, we may learn that the Common Source offers a new paradigm of cooperation and integration. The Common Source offers a path away from dualism and is free from all duality. The dualistic perception and interpretation of the world is the basis of widespread division and the concept of superiority/ inferiority. Thus, the theory or model of duality can be dangerous, because it can destroy our ability to recognize our interconnected relationship with each other, the earth, Spirit and the Common Source. Dualism can destroy our ability to see that everybody and

---

[11] Tu, Wei Ming, Address to the 7th World Assembly of World Conference on Religion and Peace, Amman, Jordan, November 1999.

everything has an *equal* place in the universe and that the circle of life connects us all.

If we share this principle of the Common Source, it will be an ethical responsibility of the world religions to overcome hatred and conflict. This is an alternative worldview that meets on common ground. Dialogue among religions has provided a significant opportunity to learn about our different languages, cultures, rituals, traditions, value systems, history and text. In this process, many people recognize the Common Source of different paths and expressions and the commonality among different religious traditions.

In a small global village, religious people should be self-critical of their own traditions and reinterpret their teachings in order to reeducate their constituencies for a new era. More and more people now recognize this Common Source with increased in-depth inter-religious understanding and experience.

Hope and Vision

Religion can become a powerful and positive spiritual source in developing a hope and vision for humanity. As one of the key pillars of any society, religious leaders and people are in a powerful position to initiate a universal transformation. Universally, religion is a source of guidance, encouragement and hope when humanity undergoes extreme difficulty and hardships. Religion has a great capacity to serve humanity, as it is a leading influence on the values of billions of people in every part of the world.

The Common Source may provide needed vision and hope for a universal and even cosmic interdependence to bring people of all continents, all races and all religions together to face a common future. This ethic of oneness should be the ethic of the world's religions. Therefore, it is critical to increase dialogue among the world's religions in order to promote deeper understanding and cooperation. The world's great religions must practice this ethic to prevent hatred, bias, prejudice and narrow-mindedness against other religions and traditions. It is also necessary to have intra-religious dialogue to reduce conflict within religions. It can be enriched through a more experiential approach instead of dialogue about theology. When you experience Oneness yourself through religious practice and dialogue, it may be easier to discover the same message from many different traditions. If you study the mysticism of each religion, you can find this Common Source. The leaders of great religions and also their people must communicate with each other to build a new civilization. This approach is new and has not been engaged in before. Spiritual practice may reestablish connection with the common founding message and practical administration of all religions.

When people discover their inherent spiritual natures, they will naturally acquire more tolerance and respect for their fellow human beings. Thus, a return to spirituality will foster the spirit of cooperation and friendship that, sadly, is lacking too often in our world family. This spirituality is vital if we are to achieve our goal of living harmoniously and productively together.

The cultivation of mind increases inner spiritual qualities, which in turn enhance the ethic of Oneness. In this process, we nourish ethical consciousness. There is a growing willingness and awareness of the need to cooperate on survival and the building of a global community. By expressing our moral concerns and undertaking action we can ensure that religion becomes a powerful and positive impact on modern society. Inner spiritual civilization will verify the meanings and values of external material civilization. This will contribute to the establishment of a peaceful, productive, and integrated society.

Spiritual, ethical and educational development will lead to an inclusive worldview. It is imperative for humanity to learn to cooperate and coexist peacefully, respecting all forms of life. It is crucial that religious communities follow the message of their founders to unite for peace on earth in order to strengthen spiritual and moral leadership. It is the shared responsibility of all religions to enrich the quality of life on earth.

ONE EARTH FAMILY: ENVIRONMENTAL PARADIGM

Regardless of their race, class, color, gender, culture or religion all human beings share One planet home. We need to practice this interdependency to see all forms of life as our extended family.

Chung-san

Triple Universal Ethics, 1961

The 21st century will put humanity on trial to determine if humans can reverse the trends of the last thousand years; if humans can modify their standards of living in order to assure the health of the planet; and if we restore harmony between humans and nature.

Humanity's pace of awakening to the true reality of the environmental crisis is too slow. Many parts of the world face severe water shortages due to drought while other locations are experiencing excessive rainfall. For the Northern Hemisphere summer temperatures, in recent decades appear to be the warmest since at least 1400 AD.[12] The average sea level has

---

[12] National Oceanic and Atmospheric Administration, *Global Warming,* Dec. 1999.

been rising at a rate of 1 to 2 mm/year over the past 100 years, which is significantly larger than the average rate over the last thousand years."[13] Humanity is responsible for dumping between 1-10 billion gallons of oil into the ocean each year.[14] Only 10% of this toxic oil is removed from the ocean,[15] the result is that natural food chains are systemically destroyed and the balance of the earth is profoundly offset. The rapid growth of urbanization is causing massive air pollution. Over 80 per cent of the planet's forests have been destroyed or degraded; a quarter of the world's mammal species is at serious risk of extinction; and biological diversity is disappearing at an alarming rate. The world's population has now passed six billion, and 1.2 billion live on less than $1 a day. Meanwhile, the share of the planet's resources being used by the affluent minority is growing and this excessive consumption of the minority is driving the forces of environmental degradation.[16]

Environmental crisis is related to our inner state of mind. We create our world by attitudes and perceptions. Our inner state of mind is then projected onto the outer world. We, therefore, must deal with inner conflicts, divisions, struggles and egocentrism before they threaten to engulf the world that we live in. We need to recognize the power of prayer and need for spiritual healing to overcome our human frailties.

We are urgently in need of a new more inclusive worldview that embraces all forms of life and a new ethic. The Triple Universal Ethics are new ethics toward the Earth. Chung-san's concept of One Family includes all forms of life

---

[13] *Ibid.*
[14] *Ibid.*
[15] *Ibid.*
[16] Klaus Toepfer, Message of UNEP Executive Director on the World Environment Day, 5 June 2000.

based on his worldview of creative interconnectedness and interdependence. It is an ecological paradigm. Environmental crisis calls for humanity to find new solutions collectively. Ethical and spiritual crises have led to our ecological crisis.

The Triple Universal Ethics provide the ethical and spiritual basis for an inclusive worldview that all forms of life are interdependent as One Family on One planet Earth. For example, if vegetation does not produce oxygen, no human can survive even a few hours. Similarly an infant cannot survive without its parents. We are fundamentally interdependent with each other. This ethic of the earth community will help us to treat all forms of life as our extended family. The inner ethic of spiritual development and meditation are not only for personal salvation but also for collective progress through ecological awareness of this profound interdependency.

Buddhists see the world as interdependent and interconnected. Won Buddhists see this linkage of interdependency as "the Four Graces": The Grace of Heaven and Earth, Parents, the Earth Community, and the True Law. Two out of the Four Graces, the Grace of Heaven and Earth and the Grace of Earth Community are directly related to environmental issues. Indifference to the ecological crisis can only occur when human beings fail to recognize the interdependence and interrelationship of all beings.

A world of interdependence requires a world of vital involvement. Since what we do touches all beings in an interdependent world, we are compelled to act in a manner that will benefit all.

Overcoming Western Dualism

Our ecological crisis has strong roots in philosophy and religion. The material world of nature has been devalued by some religions. The worldview associated with the Western Abrahamic traditions of Judaism, Christianity and Islam has created a dominantly human-focused morality. Western worldviews have tended to see nature as a commodity to be consumed by humans.

The Triple Universal Ethics emphasizes that all forms of life are based on a common origin. This belief helps us to overcome dominant Western dualism. Dualism results in domination because it tends to lead to the falsely established superiority of one part over the other. This dualism has been a foundation of major global problems including sexism, racism, classism, and environmental degradation.

The ecological crisis is connected to the basic dualism at the root of Western civilization, philosophy and technology. Divisions between spiritual and physical, mind and body, humans and nature, ourselves and others, and men and women create an unbalanced, unhealthy society in which crisis arises. Thus, the task of solving global issues is to forge a genuinely holistic worldview.

Non-dualism lends support to interconnected entities because it does not allow for domination or prioritization of one over another. This philosophy will bring to an end a past defined by darkness, conflict, domination and discrimination.

Human's specific behaviors reflect their worldviews. If a society's dominant worldview is dualism, all its institutions will reflect this philosophy. The core problems within societies, such as sexism, racism and environmental degradation are reflections of a dualistic worldview. The ethic of Common Source overcomes the divisive difficulties of dualism.

Personal and Social Transformation

Ethics of One Earth Family will be recognized through spiritual transformation. This personal transformation will recognize the intrinsic goodness of humanity. Cultivation of the mind will awaken human capacity and dignity. Our mind controls our thoughts, which determines our actions thus our destinies. If we want to change our reality, we must change our thought patterns that will result in new beliefs and actions.

In general human beings are spiritual beings that seek meaning and value in their existence on earth. Humans have great potentials, which are not fully developed. Spirituality is a great source to cultivate authentic power. Spiritual cultivation will deepen and strengthen our inner life, inspiration, peace, wisdom and compassion. These essential elements will meet the challenges of the global society. Spiritual cultivation is essential to human survival as a whole.

Buddhists believe that all humans have a light within, the divine Buddha Nature that can lead to attainment of enlightenment. Therefore we must spend part of our life in silence and meditation to discover this Inner Light. Then this light must be translated into our daily life. Through mind-cultivation, we can channel our positive energy, and bring forth our inherent goodness and universal compassion. Through meditation we reduce our own suffering, and also reduce others' suffering. Mind-cultivation leads us to self-discipline and self-transformation and enables us to practice love and compassion for all. It fuels the process of spiritual rejuvenation for the greatest benefit to individual and all forms of life.

Meditation and cultivation of the mind are imperative for our survival in this rapidly changing world. Indeed, the human mind-heart has a capacity for both universal compassion and destructive cruelty. The mind-heart is therefore the source of both good and evil.[17] Global trends that result in death and destruction are the result of negative and ignorant thought patterns and corresponding unbalanced actions. Destructive thought cycles have resulted in repeated genocidal wars throughout human history. The negative thought trends create vicious dualistic archetypes of victims and victimizing, and the oppressed and the oppressor.

Today human-centered materialism increases suffering of other forms of life such as animals and plants. We are destroying our own future. The elimination of suffering is the ultimate concern of conscious people. Human behavior can be evaluated in terms of its capacity to promote or reduce suffering of all forms. Human beings create suffering because of greed, anger and ignorance. It is apparent that greed, hatred and ignorance in their various manifestations are also the factors that generate insecurity among people. We must seek to improve our earth community by improving ourselves as individuals first and then trying to change social structures to reverse our trends. The path to enlightenment includes overcoming these forces through spiritual practice. Such practice will deepen human relationships with other forms of life. It is within our control to allow, "favor to arise from harm or harm from favor." [18]

Through personal transformation we recognize a common origin with others. Then we begin to take care of the planet earth as our own home and treat all forms of life as our own extended family. The concept of One Earth Family based on interconnectedness and interdependency is the ethic of ecology

---

[17] *The Scripture of Won Buddhism*, 307.
[18] *Ibid.*, 6.

and serves as a new environmental paradigm. Social transformation and personal transformation are deeply interrelated. If enough individuals transform themselves, it will be possible to influence social transformation. Any form of meaningful change must have both dimensions of inner transformation and outer change. We cannot commit ourselves to the common good if the forces of personal greed, hatred, anger or delusion overwhelm us. At the same time, we cannot find personal liberation if we ignore the suffering of others. Ecological imbalance alerts us to be mindful of the ethic of Oneness to bring harmony between humans and nature. Thus, indifference to the ecological crisis can only occur when human beings fail to recognize the interrelationship of all beings.

The needed social transformation requires educational and media institutions to be redesigned in order to bring more accurate multicultural and inclusive knowledge and information. These are societal pillars that directly impact people's perceptions and thus their value systems and actions.

In educational institutions, textbook reform that depicts a more inclusive, truthful version of history is imperative. Schools are the institutions of self-cultivation and leadership development. In order for everybody to gain empowerment from knowing the roots of history sculpted by role models who have come before us, we must move beyond the male focus that dominates the majority of school textbooks today.

The media is a powerful tool and a part of the check and balance system in a democracy. It is important to ensure that the freedom of journalists and media outlets is maintained. It is important to ensure the framework and structure of the media is composed of and run by a demographic that is reflective of the population it serves. Every culture, gender, class and race has a different perspective that is invaluable to integrate into the media.

Principle of Cause and Effect

Science and common sense have taught us that for every action, there is an equal and opposite reaction. In Buddhism, this relationship is interpreted as the Principle of Cause and Effect. One example of this is that because of the abuse of the environment, earth's inhabitants must now endure the detrimental consequences.

We are influenced by all life around us. Our mood is influenced by others' moods and our well being is deeply interconnected with the well being of life around us. It is critical to recognize that when we advance others we advance ourselves as well. Therefore, we need to practice the principle of mutual interest instead of calculated self-interest, mutual prosperity instead of aggressive egoism. We need a greater sense of openness to each other, which encourages self-discipline, self-reliance, spirituality, self-reflection, mutual respect, trust, and understanding toward a new civilization.

It is our moral obligation to adopt a new way of living in order to pursue sustainable development and safeguard the global commons. It becomes an essential goal to reform our wasteful lifestyles. Also we need to create legislation to protect our extended family of life system. In this way we protect the future of coming generations.

Due to the principle of cause and effect, we will pay for the consequences in whatever we do. When we are capable of practicing love and compassion for all based on the principle of cause and effect, we can hopefully expand our sense of community and family to include all living beings. A more mature humanity will awaken to the truth of cause and effect, that we reap what we sow. Therefore we must be responsible for ourselves at the same time responsible for everything else and everyone else around us.

We are called to unite as One Family to support a sustainable and harmonious relationship between human species and nature. Respect for life is vital to the well being of any society. The sanctity of life is a concept shared by people of all religions and spiritual traditions as well as by secular humanists. Each diverse form of life has its own intrinsic value. All forms of life embody beauty inspiring human consciousness with wonder, joy and creativity.

Human beings have a special moral obligation to preserve life in its integrity. We are the ones who have heaped the destructive forces of imbalance and environmental degradation upon the earth, our children and ourselves. Our concern for the earth community should be expressed in action, in our personal, professional and political lives as well as in statements of principles. We must have the wisdom and willingness to reestablish a better relationship between this earth and its people, between humans and other living beings.

Human beings need to grow in the spiritual life, to balance the material life. They also must balance economic and environmental needs by means of the spiritual teachings of balance, equilibrium and contentment. This leads to a simple, disciplined way of life.

ONE WORK PLACE: GLOBAL INTERDEPENDENCY

All enterprises in the world should participate in building a better world. All humanity should recognize the ultimate relationship with the large whole.

Chungsan

Triple Universal Ethics

Today's world and its problems are becoming increasingly more interdependent and interconnected due to globalization and advancement of science and technology. Interdependency of the whole world can change into a social, economic, nuclear, or environmental catastrophe. The magnitude of these problems requires all human beings to work together in finding new solutions.

The need for spiritual guidance is evident as we reflect on how our civilization has succumbed, from time to time, to the human frailties of greed, ambition, xenophobic myopia, and selfishness. We have seen that heinous acts are often committed under the veil of public mandates when in fact they are the wishes of the few in power, be they economic, political, military, or even religious. At other times, atrocities are committed out of a mistaken fear of the unknown.

The planet earth has put humanity on trial. The trial is whether we can transform ourselves from self-interest to the common good, whether humanity can cooperate on a global scale to overcome the ecological crisis, widespread poverty, and nuclear disaster, and whether international institutions can incorporate ethical and spiritual values in the global affairs. In these global scale trials, human beings must learn to be co-workers by recognizing One Work Place on One planet. In order for humanity to pass these trials, we need more creativity and global solidarity.

If we understand the Common Source, we will practice this ethic of One Work Place. All different professionals and endeavors will find the common purpose. This common purpose will bring the spirit of cooperation to the One Work Place. We have to help people to live well with others in order to live well ourselves.

It is a challenge for humanity to learn to become co-workers on earth. Is it possible to find some approach amongst social, economic, political and religious, philosophical, and scientific disciplines? It is possible that they may search for the same truth. As co-workers in One Work Place professionals have many different talents and skills to build a home of love and justice for all.

We must combine our different but equally important resources to foster global solidarity. Unless this spirit of cooperation flourishes, our world community will once again experience the tragic consequences of wars, environmental disasters, and moral deterioration. With practice of the ethic of cooperation in a common purpose, all social, political and religious, philosophical, scientific, economic enterprises must utilize their vast and unique resources.

The United Nations: A Common Purpose

The United Nations is the only existing global institution with universal membership. One of the purposes of the United Nations is to maintain international peace and security, to develop friendly relations among nations based on respect for the principles of equal rights and self-determination. Other major purposes of the United Nations is:

To achieve international cooperation in solving

international problems of an economic, social, cultural, or
humanitarian character, and in promoting and encouraging
respect for human rights and for fundamental freedoms for
all without distinction as to race, sex, language or
religion.[19]

The United Nations is a center for harmonizing the actions
of nations in the attainment of these common ends. The
Charter has its basis in spiritual values. The UN is an essential
world organization, which embodies our hopes for a more just
and humane future. The Charter recognizes the importance of
global unity in achieving a healthy, just, and harmonious world.
The organization upholds ideals of equality and respect,
community and selflessness. The Charter also contains noble
and spiritual values such as human dignity.

In its fifty-five years of existence, the UN has struggled to
accomplish it's purposes. With much success, the United
Nations has combated disease and increased world literacy. It
has provided millions living in poverty with food and basic
medicine. And year after year, the General Assembly
continues to adopt resolutions aimed at combating strife and
oppression with international compassion and action. Yet while
these declarations embody the UN Charter's ideals, the
effectiveness of implementing them has been limited. Now
members of the global community are attempting to reform the
United Nations.

In any reform process, the United Nations needs shared
philosophical and ethical principles. The Triple Universal
Ethics provides a strong spiritual and ethical base with which
to actualize the Charter of the United Nations. We the people
of the United Nations have a Common Purpose and Common

---

[19] *The Charter of the United Nations*, 4.

Principle as One Earth Family to live well individually and to create a better world collectively. By considering the ethical, moral and spiritual dimensions of the mission of the United Nations, unprecedented change can occur. True change must come willingly from within.[20] It will allow the United Nations to address the root causes of the global problems it is charged with solving.

The United Nations needs to cooperate more with religious communities. Dealing with human mind-heart the world' religions can strengthen the world organization. Religious representatives at the United Nations can take the initiative in making concerted efforts to provide the spiritual guidance for all members of this world family. We may utilize the power of prayer and spiritual healing to develop a peaceful world community.

A minute of silence for prayer or meditation should be extended to all meetings of the United Nations. The best way members of the General Assembly can heighten their own consciousness and foster spirituality is through the power of meditation and prayer. Rule 62 of the Rules of Procedure of the General Assembly provides:

> Immediately after the opening of the first plenary meeting and immediately preceding the closing of the final meeting of each session of the General Assembly, the president shall invite the representative to observe one minute of silence dedicated to prayer or meditation.[21]

Through prayer or meditation representatives from all

---

[20] Universal Ethics Millennium Conference, Summary Report, April 12, 2000.

[21] United Nations, The Rules of Procedure of the General Assembly

nations center their minds on the job in the beginning of each meeting with the goal of deepening their wisdom. At the end of each meeting a minute of silence permits them to reflect on their achievements and failures. Ambassadors and representatives need time to reflect on their work which can indirectly and dramatically affect millions of people.

The world is moving toward a new, more participatory, people-centered way of conducting international affairs. The Triple Universal Ethics can be one of the spiritual foundations in reforming the United Nations.

Critical Role of Women in a New Civilization

The inner spiritual life force is a source of power useful in overcoming external difficulties. The feminist movement reflects the utilization of this spiritual power. Traditionally, women in many cultures were taught that subordination and endurance were womanly virtues that they should strive for. Women were thus subtly persuaded into silence. Furthermore, the silence of the world community in the face of gender inequality has been deafening. Our potential for inner silence, however, can be a positive force, a pulsating, healing power. Contemplative silence and the silence of compassionate listening are very positive. Silence in meditation can be the power that heals the wounds that other silences inflict and the power that leads to the discovery of the divinity within, the Buddha Nature in every one of us. Through silent meditation, we discover ourselves and learn to use our own wisdom, our own Truth, and our own inner strength. Likewise, the global problems force us to go deeper into our spiritual source and develop our inner life to meet global challenges.

Article 18 of the Universal Declaration of Human Rights proclaims the right to freedom of thought, conscience, and religion. This right belongs not to a chosen few but to all people. Without freedom of thought, conscience and religion, a human cannot develop the highest potential to function appropriately in our complicated society. However women's rights to freedom of thought, conscience and religion have been oppressed due to patriarchal values. Women's thoughts are often ignored. Women's conscience is considered as inferior. Women's religion is repeatedly denied. Economically, socially, and politically women suffer from inequality. Women constitute over half the world's population, perform nearly two-thirds of its work hours, receive one-tenth of the world's income, own less than one-tenth of the world's property, and hold 1 percent of chief executive position worldwide. [22] Physically, mentally and spiritually, women face enormous consequences of discrimination.

Women's perspectives should be included in all levels of decision making. A woman's movement at international, national and local levels can be useful in solving global problems. The women's liberation movement is one of the strongest cultural trends of our time. As it has grown, this movement has come to influence all facets of society. Feminists believe that all existing institutions must be reformed or restructured to restore full dignity of all forms of life.

The United Nations needs to place more women at the center of the decision-making process as equal partners with men. This process may contribute to bringing people together cooperatively. Women's active contribution is vital to conflict resolution, population, environment, social development, human rights and all other enterprises. There is hope because

---

[22] Noeleen Heyzer, ed. *A Commitment to the World's Women*, (United Nations Development Fund for Women, 1995), 2.

members of the United Nations are increasingly recognizing the importance of women's rights, and their effects on socio-economic development as a whole.

It is critical to invite the active role of women in building a new civilization because at the present time half of the population's talents are wasted. If we fully incorporate women's gifts, humanity will be enabled to build a balanced new global civilization. The full potentials of women must be utilized.

Dialogue among Civilizations

In the emerging era, clashes of civilizations are the greatest threat to world peace, and international order based on civilizations is the surest safeguard against world war.

Samuel P. Huntington

The Clash of Civilizations, 1997

Dialogue is a peaceful and ethical approach to conflict among different cultures, perspectives, worldviews, and ideologies. Due to increasing globalization, there is a higher possibility of different cultures, religions and civilizations encountering each other. It is apparent therefore that the most urgent priority facing our multicultural world today is to find creative peaceful solutions to today's problems, together.

Dialogue among Civilizations may provide a significant opportunity to discuss root causes of global problems. Civilizations change and adapt when they encounter new cultures. The history of civilization shows us that human relations break down when different perspectives, worldviews, ideologies and cultures come into confrontation.[23] The key to human survival in this era of increasing globalization is learning how to cope creatively with the powerful forces that arise when diverse civilizations clash.

Our intercultural, interreligious and international experiences elevate us to a higher global perspective. Each diverse civilization can contribute to the global village if it engages in a constructive dialogue with the others and if it learns from the other. Dialogue among different ideologies, philosophies and worldviews may contribute to transform, mature and adopt new values to survive together. Diverse civilizations may provide different perspectives and methods for common problems. All civilizations can learn from each other to face the common future. This dialogue must pay attention to minority voices. New solutions and approaches may be drawn from these previously unheard voices. The twenty-first century calls for more discussion among civilizations, religions, cultures, ideologies and worldviews. It requires more interdisciplinary approaches. Dialogue among Civilizations needs to include a dialogue among all different professionals who have different skills and talents to contribute to humanity.

We may find convergence among different cultures and ideologies. Dialogue among Civilizations can pursue the Ethic of One Work Place to deal with global issues. This ethic inspires us to transform self-centeredness in order to practice the principle of mutual interest. When we practice the ethic of One Work Place, we would balance common good and individual good. The principle of mutual interest and common good will motivate political, economic, technological,

---

[23] Global Dialogue Institute.

scientific, moral and spiritual contributions to create a new civilization for everyone's benefits.

Dialogue among Civilizations at the United Nations could lead to the establishment of a *Universal Group* representing all major sectors of society. A new civilization will bring integration and convergence. This integration can be developed through dialogues among different professionals including academics, diplomats, staffs, agencies, religious communities, Non-Governmental Organizations, political experts, the business community, journalists, scientists, medical professionals and other civil society groups. In the future, all professionals must work together to search for new solutions. It will be crucial for humanity to search for a Common Source and a Common Purpose through an interdisciplinary approach.

Dialogue among Civilizations, based on the ethic of One Work Place, can offer a forum to learn how to live side by side in peaceful interaction and interchange. This dialogue invites humanity to study and exchange accomplishments in religion, art, literature, philosophy, science, technology, morality and compassion of the world's great civilizations in order to enrich each other's lives.

CONCLUSION

Although the most important changes generally begin within ourselves, they must eventually be translated into changes in community, national and global institutions. We must be mindful of the changes needed at all these levels and contribute to their realization.[24]

David C. Korten

The Post-Corporate World, 1999

We are concerned with the spiritual, political, environmental and social welfare of the entire life system. We have ample wealth and technology on earth currently, but do not have a sense of consciousness great enough to share and distribute these resources. To meet the global challenges, it requires rethinking and renewing of spiritual and ethical values in our local, national and global institutions. Humanity must raise consciousness to see the Common Source and recognize the One Earth Family in order to share the spiritual and material wealth.

Human capacities offer a clear choice between universal compassion and destructive cruelty. The heart-mind is the source of both good and evil.[25] When we carefully examine how we make decisions, we can say our mind creates everything. As the Charter of UNESCO stresses, war begins in

---

[24] David C. Korten, *The Post Corporate World*, (Berrett-Koehler & Kumanian Press: San Francisco, 1999), 266.

[25] *The Scripture of Won Buddhism*, 307.

the minds of men. Therefore, it is critical to cultivate our minds through meditation, reflection, education and dialogue. Mind-cultivation is an essential step to create a brighter future toward a new civilization. Hence, we are required to spend more time in meditation and silence to restore our intrinsic goodness. Universal compassion and intrinsic goodness will strengthen spiritual and ethical values to deal with global problems.

Now is the time to translate our words, vision, and ideas into actions. In this age of overwhelming material and technological advancement, we face the risk of a dwindling tide of spirituality. Science has developed technology that can connect the whole world. But only ethical and spiritual values can instill in us the wisdom to choose how to use the technology and material wealth, either for selfish purposes of power and prestige, or for the good of the whole. Maintaining balance and harmony between material and spiritual values in our individual and collective lives is imperative in building a new civilization.

The present global problems cannot be solved by an excessive dependency upon science and economics. We need to deal with the root cause of the problems. The root cause is a lack of development of the spiritual and ethical dimension. We need spirituality in action. Humanity needs to join in faithful practice to cultivate a new civilization. We must work together to incorporate spirituality back into our daily lives and collective endeavors if we are to create a better world. Through the Triple Universal Ethics endowed with spirituality, we may build a new civilization with a renewed commitment.

EPILOGUE

We have come to the end of this book. We thank you, the Reader, for accompanying us as we presented to you our ideas, reflections and suggestions from a variety of perspectives. We hope that you have found them worthy of your time and attention.

Although each one of us dealt with specific aspects of the new civilization, from the angle of our individual discipline, we wish to assure you that all of us share basic ideas, values, principles and philosophies that form the structural foundations of this book.

Thus, we are convinced that the new century is witnessing some unprecedented and fundamental inner and outer transformations at the individual and collective levels, and that in order to respond adequately to the unfolding challenges and crises of the new times, individuals, communities, and nations must display a new vision.

We are of the view that the world needs to realize that the time has come to go beyond assumptions and approaches that worked in the past and that appear to be inadequate for the new times. We believe therefore that it is becoming increasingly evident that these critical times require imagination, creativity, and the willingness to forego some old assumptions and prejudices and to have the courage to initiate and to try new ideas and approaches.

It is with this perspective in mind that we have endeavored to present to you jointly our individual views and analyses, as a common contribution to the understanding of the various aspects of the New Civilization slowly arising on the horizon.

We believe that the New Millennium will be characterized by a heightened awareness of the fundamental importance of ethics and values in the lives of individuals, communities and nations.

We further believe that humankind must treat its environment as sacred, respect and reconcile itself with the natural world, and endeavor to live harmoniously with it and within it.

At the same time, we witness that the civil society is increasingly playing a fundamental role at the local, national, and global level, and we anticipate that in the new century it will play a crucial role in shaping the local, national, and global policies.

We are confident that, as the new civilization unfolds, humankind will create the appropriate frameworks and institutions capable of embodying spiritual values. We see the world integrating slowly but perceptibly, and humanity concomitantly building new institutions to meet the exigencies of the new age.

We are certain that the new century will require an unprecedented degree of cooperation between nations and groups of nations and within global organizations and that new forms of cooperation will emerge as the process of globalization advances and the "servers" of interdependence becomes strong.

We believe that humanity can overcome the major challenges confronting it if the individuals, communities and national governments approach the problems from a cooperative perspective based on the values of respect, genuine dialogue and mutual understanding.

We are confident that humanity is capable of ascending to

higher levels of progress, both material and spiritual and we look at the future with a sense of commitment and optimism.

We hope that the ideas and reflections contained in this book could be seen as our humble contribution to that progress.